THE
CHRISTMAS PRESENCE

John Scally

THE COLUMBA PRESS

DUBLIN

First published in 2015 by
THE COLUMBA PRESS
55A Spruce Avenue
Stillorgan Industrial Park
Blackrock
Co. Dublin
Ireland
www.columba.ie

ISBN: 978-1-78218-254-2

Set in Baskerville 10/14
Book design by Helene Pertl | The Columba Press
Origination by The Columba Press
Printed by ScandBook AB, Sweden

CONTENTS

To the memory of
Ivor Dada and Cathy Burlingham
who are much missed.

Foreword
by Peter McVerry

I hate Christmas time. That may be a strange thing to hear a Catholic priest say about the celebration of what I believe to be the most significant event in the history of humankind. But it is a time of terrible financial pressure on families, particularly poorer families, some of whom may not yet have paid off the loans they had borrowed the previous Christmas. Advertisements for Christmas gifts, trying to get people to spend money they often don't have, begin in September or even earlier. Christmas is the busiest time of the year for retailers – the more we spend the happier the Minister for Finance will be – and Christmas Day is not even over when the advertisements for the January sales are beamed into every home.

I don't recognise Christmas any more. By Christmas, I mean that celebration of the birth, in a field, of the son of a poor carpenter who came to reveal to us the true meaning of life. I mean the all-powerful, all-loving God, who came among us, not as a mighty king, with power and wealth, expecting to be served, nor as a famous religious guru with a mass following, but as an unknown, powerless infant, totally dependent on the love and care of those around him. The God whose life and death has revealed to us the true meaning of our own life and death.

This book helps us to escape for a while from the madness of Christmas today to bring us back to the Christmas of 2,000 years ago. Simple stories, but with a depth of meaning; short stories, which take only a few minutes to read, but a lifetime to assimilate; stories which capture the imagination of children aged six to ninety-six and open our eyes to realities beyond the tinsel and the turkey.

In this book, we are invited to stand still for a while and ponder the true meaning of Christmas. It should be compulsory reading for everyone before we rush off to do our Christmas shopping.

Introduction

As a boy growing up in Roscommon, Christmas really began in earnest on 'Big Saturday', the Saturday before Christmas, when we journeyed into town to 'bring home the Christmas'. It was far and away the busiest day in the town, a fascinating mixture of the Christmas spirit and hard-nosed business. For me, the big task was to buy seven presents with a solitary pound note in my pocket, the fruit of three months' saving, though setting out that morning I thought I had a fortune. A set of four hair-combs for my grandmother, a half-dozen razor blades for my grandfather, a box of multicoloured soaps for my mother and sweets for my sisters made up my shopping list.

In the centre of the square a group of tuneless singers made up a raucous street choir, managing to turn the timeless classic 'Silent Night' into a contradiction in terms. As they were trying to raise money for St Vincent de Paul and it was the season of goodwill to all men and women, I felt obliged to give them a shiny thrupenny piece.

The Christmas mince was always bought in 'Cheap Joe's', pronounced locally as 'Chape Joe's'. His shop was down a side alley almost hidden away and it was so tiny that there was hardly room to swing a cat. It was full. It was always full on market days and this being Big Saturday it was packed out.

The Holy Grail

The highlight of the day was a visit to the biggest shop in town to see Santa Claus. The toyshop was like an Aladdin's cave to my spellbound eyes. I always loved the way the little bell went 'ching' as I opened the door. Armed with a shining two-shilling piece – a gift from my grandfather and the requisite fee for the honour of receiving Santa – I took my place in the queue in a state of high excitement. On one occasion I was very surprised to see a retired nun, who visited our school from time to time to help prepare the pupils for First Holy Communion, in the queue. She was with three small children of the travelling family in our parish, who lived in a big tent by the side of the road.

A few months earlier, one of their older brothers had been responsible for a spate of petty thefts and some destruction of property and would as a consequence be spending his Christmas in jail. The family had been shunned by the local community in the following months. They were refused entry to local pubs and shops. At Sunday Mass they sat together on the back seat of the church. None of the 'upright' pillars of the community would sit on the same seat as them. A few of the more superior parishioners decided to go to Mass in the neighbouring parish. Even then I thought that there were was a curious irony in coming together to worship and listen to the word of God calling for love of neighbour and at the same time deliberately ignoring a neighbour. The eloquence of the words did not translate into practical action.

At that stage of my life I had one all-consuming ambition in my life, which was to emulate my hero, Roscommon's greatest ever footballer, Dermot Earley, and lead my county to innumerable wins on the sporting field. For this reason, I was going to ask Santa for a pair of football boots and a football. However, my plans were modified when I got my first lesson in social awareness hearing Santa's conversation with Brian, the youngest of the travelling children who was just ahead of me in the queue.

'Now little boy what will I bring you for Christmas?'

'Please sir, would ya bring me a nice dry blanket to keep me warm on the cauld nights?'

How could I possibly ask for two presents after that? I just asked for a football and did not complain that I had got poor value for my two shillings when Santa handed me a cheap-looking colouring book.

The Big Smoke

Up to Big Saturday we always felt jealous of the McElvies. Their entire family went up to Dublin on the eighth of December, the Feast of the Immaculate Conception, when Dublin was invaded by the culchies. Listening to Mark McElvie talk about the day it seemed like Heaven. I knew every detail of the day as well as if I had made the journey myself. They travelled by train from Athlone in the morning darkness, an event in itself, with the stops in all the little towns and the commuters coming and going like buzzing bees, the struts, smoke and sparks as the powerful engine clicketty-clacked to the capital city. The lucky ones grabbed the window seat and marvelled at the flashing world as the sky got lighter until it was broad daylight.

Then there was Dublin itself with its fascinating mix of majestic and ugly buildings, the tiny shops and the big stores and the sombre, sinister Liffey flowing silently all the way. The first shop to be visited was always Switzers, the shop whose window was populated with glorious gnomes who moved rhythmically to the sound of accompanying music. Crowds gathered, young and old, men and women, just to savour the innocence of it all. Switzers was also where the four McElvie children went to see Santa Claus. This was something special, like a trip to Fairyland, a glorious treat that would repay all the weeks of being good.

Then it was off to the Gresham Hotel to be pampered for dinner. It seemed so posh, having a real Christmas dinner before Christmas came at all. The first course had to be a huge bowl of chicken soup and the obligatory two slices of fresh brown bread complete with generous helpings of creamy butter. The normal impatience of waiting between courses was suspended in such palatial and privileged surroundings. The main course consisted of Christmas turkey, ham, sprouts, peas and roast potatoes. Mouth-watering Christmas pudding covered with a liberal dollop of bright yellow, thin-flowing custard made up the afters. Every bite was savoured in this regal atmosphere.

An hour and a half was spent in the hotel; then it was out to get down to the more serious business of Christmas shopping. This was not as easy as it sounded, as all the better-off people in rural Ireland had congregated in Dublin for the same purpose and all had targeted the prestigious shops like Clerys to make their purchases. There was barely room to sneeze. In the toyshops, doll's houses, draughts, snakes and ladders were doing a roaring trade. In the bookshops, Mills and Boone and Enid Blyton were the popular choices, with my favourites 'The Hardy Boys' and Biggles doing well also. The Beatles, Elvis Presley and Cliff Richard battled it out with Irish artists like Dermot O'Brien and The Dubliners in the record shops. The shop doors were continually opening, with the steady flow of bargain hunters, though some were there only to browse.

Then it was back to Heuston station for the 5 p.m. train home, arms laden with gift-wrapped Christmas presents as the Dublin dusk descended. The enduring image was always of the Christmas lights in O'Connell Street. The simplicity of the lights was always more magical than the more ornate decorations. The journey home was shortened by the consumption of a big bag of fudge and lovely creamy buns, shaped like a butterfly. It all seemed so real to me – but I never visited Dublin on the eighth of December as a child. Matt McElvie's descriptions were so vivid I felt I walked every step of the journey with him.

Ritual

Big Saturday was our substitute for going to Dublin. Grandpa had lit a fire when we got home. Although the light was off, the fire gave leaping flames, dancing shadows and a rosy glow. On Big Saturday night the decorations were always put up. The Christmas tree was normally the first to be decorated. After great debate the nicest cards we had received were selected and exhibited on the mantelpiece amidst a sea of tinsel and holly. We cheated by putting two rows of string across the ceiling and hanging up the nicest cards from previous years. A turnip was carefully chosen to play reluctant host to a tall white Christmas candle, which was neatly adorned with sprigs of red berry holly and dispatched on the kitchen windowsill.

A birth like no other

The Sunday before Christmas was always the day for setting up the crib. My job had always been to look after the three characters who represented the Magi, but this year was to be different. My mother said to me: 'You're the artistic one. You do the crib.' I made a stable comprised of four stout twigs and a thatched roof.

The crib gave me an agonising insight into the minds and hearts of the characters of the first Christmas. The story was old yet new each year. I never failed to wonder at the wonderful: how God took time to enter human history. The baby's life was one of contradiction even at birth, because a young girl, still a virgin, gave him life. His birth was so significant that even the stars were thrown into rapture and subservience. An infant's voice was turning the world on its head. He was different in seeing evil but not being it.

Growing up on a farm, I knew that the nativity scene could not possibly have been the romantic, sweet-smelling, clean event portrayed on so many Christmas cards. Despite the great advances in farming methods and buildings, I had never been in a stable that was fit for a baby to be born. I could imagine the smells, the draughts and the scatterings of farmyard manure. This really brought home to me the hardships and discomforts of the first Christmas.

There's no one like Grandma

I often thought I had not one maternal grandmother, but at least ten. She was a multifaceted personality. She was witty, kind, potentially ruthless, charming, cool, patient, impatient, generous, economical, cautious, carefree, impulsive, far-seeing, enchanting, occasionally vicious, dour and charismatic. The list was endless. Her mood changed more often than the Irish weather.

She had a memory like an elephant. Right up to my early twenties she often reminded me of two incidents from my childhood. One was when I was three years old and had left a tap running in the bathroom, causing a minor flood to develop. The second occurred when I was seven and had foolishly brought my football into the hallway to practise my skills on a wet day. A crashing sound announced that I would never be the new George Best, as the football made contact with a holy water fountain.

Our cow, Brownie, gave my grandmother cause to be happy because she produced a phenomenal milk yield, right up to Christmas. This was important because she always made pounds of butter to give to our city cousins. My friends always knew that Christmas was coming when their mother started baking Christmas cakes and puddings, but my first clue that Christmas was coming was when I came home from school to see my grandmother with her sleeves rolled up to her elbows, working energetically at our blue-barrelled butter churn.

Christmas always brought out the child within my grandmother. On the morning of Christmas Eve she insisted that my grandfather would tidy up around the sides of the house, in case any of the reindeers might trip over anything as Santa Claus came to deliver our presents. Not a speck of dust could be left on the side of the house in case Santy got his red coat dirty when he went up on the roof to climb down the chimney. She always insisted that the chimney sweep was summoned to our house the day before Christmas Eve. We always had three chairs left around the Christmas tree for Santy to stack the presents individually for us. It was my grandmother who left a bottle of Guinness and a slice of Christmas cake on each chair. She decreed that each of us leave a letter to Santa thanking him for the presents we got last year. There was always a handwritten note for each of us with the same message every year:

> Have a nice Christmas. Be good for your Mammy next year.
> Remember I will be watching you. Don't eat too many
> sweets on Christmas Day.
> Ho, ho, ho!
> Santa

All creatures meek and tall

Christmas Eve too brought other annual rituals. That was the day when the postman was invited in for a little 'drop out of the bottle'. It was just a small symbol of the outpouring of goodness which the Christmas season triggered.

On the night before Christmas, freshly cut ivy and red-berried holly were twined about the hanging cords of the pictures on the wall. A tin of biscuits was passed among all family members, bringing a tangible air of goodwill to the household. Any disappointment about missing the nicest chocolate ones was carefully disguised. The biscuits never made it past Christmas Eve. It was a tradition every year that the tin would find a place in the corner of the back kitchen. Like my grandfather, my mother could not abide waste. The empty biscuit tin became known as the 'hen's bucket' and all food waste, sour milk, tea leaves, egg shells and potato skins ended up there. Their next destination was to be breakfast for either our hens or ducks. Tins of biscuits were a rare treat for us. Every good customer in the local post office-cum-grocer-cum-newsagent got a tin of biscuits and a calendar. It was a gesture of appreciation for patronage during the year.

In dark's dull density, the curtains were stripped off the windows and a single candle was put to burn in each sill till the morning. Once, I put up a poster saying: 'Peace and goodwill to all men and women, apart from the following exceptions...' My mother took it down immediately on the grounds that it went against the spirit of the season.

Before going to sleep we had two important tasks to complete. Firstly, we went to the chimney and shouted up the presents we wanted from Santy. Mary was terrified by the idea that anyone could get down the chimney and through the open fireplace to her own room when she was fast asleep.

Secondly, we hung up our stockings near our beds. We borrowed the biggest stockings we could find from our grandfather. They were to be filled not by Father Christmas, but by our grandparents. Anticipation was always the keenest pleasure. Bursting with impatience, we resolved to stay awake all night, to sneak a peep through the bannister, to catch a glimpse of Santa's red cloak.

The stockings were not to be touched until after the Christmas dinner. Then the presents were pulled out and examined with squeaks of delight and excitement, muffled as far as possible to let my grandfather have his customary snooze on the chair (a muffling process helped by unwrapping and eating a few bars of delicious Cadbury's chocolate). Our feet hardly touched the ground with delirium. I always thought it was a strange custom that children should hang up stockings, but no matter how hard I tried I could never find any adult I knew who would explain it to me. I understood their reticence when I discovered that the idea sprung from St Nicholas saving three beautiful sisters from a life of prostitution. He gave gifts of gold for their dowries anonymously by throwing bags of money through the windows while the girls slept, and into the stockings which were hanging ready for the morning.

The second coming

On Christmas morning we woke early, long before the first faint vestiges of light illuminated the specklings of frost on the hard ground. We rushed downstairs, drawn as if by a magnet to the place under the Christmas tree where, hopefully, Santa Claus had neatly piled our presents. Competition was intense as to who was to be the first to make the discovery, to shriek out 'He came, He came!', our shining faces a fitting reward to the idea of Santa.

We always had porridge for breakfast on Christmas morning. My mother assured me that the Celts were responsible for Christmas pudding, which started life as nothing more than a great big bowl of porridge. It was years later that I discovered that not everyone had porridge for Christmas. My mother also told me that at one stage the most hated figure in Irish history, Cromwell, had banned all Christmas festivities to prevent people from enjoying themselves. Cromwell had always been my bête noire because of his remark, which never failed to anger me: 'To hell or to Connacht.' His views on Christmas convinced me that he was not just dastardly, but daft.

At Mass that morning there was a crush of people. The standard greeting of Mass-goers to one another was 'A Happy Christmas', though some went native and said: '*Go mberimid beo ag an am seo arís'*, their breath like a plume of smoke in the frosty air. Inside, the focal point was the crib, with a big silver star shining in the roof, and a little baby so real I would not have been surprised if he began to wail in his diminutive straw manger. It did at least remind me that it was a baby, not Santa Claus, that was, is and always would be Christmas.

In the arms of the angels
The gospel always spoke of angels. I was always enthralled by the idea of angels. The pictures I saw of angels were of creatures robed in white with outspread wings, kindly smiles and celestial vision. Angels were always good but essentially heavenly. I liked them because they formed a tenuous connection with the unseen worlds and signified the greatest of mysteries: humankind's passage through time.

After Mass, preparations for the Christmas dinner began in earnest. A special tablecloth was taken out from under its hiding place and the best china and delph were rescued from the top shelf in the cupboard. The meal itself was marked by a level of courtesy and ceremony which no meal for the rest of the year could match; a small indication of this was the frequent usage of the phrase 'please pass me …' After the feast the Christmas parcels from relatives were undone. My mother made a list of distant donors so that we could write thank-you letters the following day.

God bless all here
We all received a book each. This particular year, mine was the classic *A Christmas Carol.* On the cover an evil-looking Ebenezer Scrooge, complete with hideous hat, glared defiantly at me. This revolting portrait was offset by the hypnotic sweetness of little Tim Cratchit. There was always an annual for each of us. My sister got what I considered 'cissy' annuals, *Bunty* and *Judy*, while

I usually got *Dandy*. When the novelty of the toys wore off and we had watched the Abbot and Costello film on television, we devoured our new reading material.

Looking back, I remember the Christmas of my childhood with great affection, because it nurtured the understanding of the season which remains with me to this day: as a time of mystery, magic, hope and, above all, innocence. My abiding memory of every Christmas Day is of my grandfather saying with unsurpassed eloquence after the Christmas dinner: 'Thank God for Christmas.' Only now do I appreciate the depth of meaning in that simple sentence.

In some hearts it's never Christmas

Yet even as a child I was always aware that there was a darker side to Christmas. Every year, our next-door neighbour, George, an elderly man who lived alone, joined us for dinner on Christmas Eve, and on Christmas Day he joined relatives for Christmas dinner. My mother had patiently explained to us that not everyone enjoys Christmas, particularly those who are lonely or those who have no money to buy 'nice things' for Christmas. Those of us who were the lucky ones had a special obligation to 'bring Christmas' to those who were not so fortunate.

The previous Sunday at Mass the priest had quoted somebody called Thomas Merton, who wrote: 'With those for whom there is no room is Jesus.' He went on to say:

'I like to think also that especially at Christmas: with those for whom there is no one to share their rooms is Jesus. The sad reality is that life is difficult for many people. The message of Christmas is that Christ is made flesh not in the unreal beauty of the Christmas card, but in the mess that is our world. For those of us who claim to be Christian, Christ is made flesh in our neighbours.'

At Christmas, George was melancholy, pessimistic, moody, though durable. In a peculiar way he both looked forward to the season of goodwill and dreaded it. He was impatient for the magic that never came, but that all the preparations promised. For him, Christmas was above all a time to be lonely. In his microcosm lay rural Ireland's universality. He remembered his family scattered all over the world: England Australia, America and Canada. While they felt exile, homesickness and longing and hoped for returns that would never materialise, he was trapped in a prison of memories. His pain was the piercing grief of never being able to return to the way things used to be.

He was the seventh son of a seventh son. He had what was known locally as 'the gift'. People came from miles around for him to lay his hands on them in a desperate hope that he would cure them. I had to visit him once myself in his professional capacity when I fell victim to the highly infectious rural disease called ringworm. My arm was invaded by an unsightly and maddeningly itchy scab. George placed my hand in a bowl of holy water and made the sign of the cross on it. He rubbed some kind of homemade concoction on it. It looked awful and smelt worse, but it took away the itch and stopped me scratching. Within five days I was cured.

God rest ye merry gentlemen
George was a small, slight man. In many ways he was a child who had never grown up. He was a great talker and was au fait with the local gossip, though he had neither viciousness nor bitterness. He loved a good yarn but was never unduly bothered about trifles like veracity. If the truth had to be adapted to suit the story he had no problems with it. My grandfather always said: 'George says more than his prayers.'

I remember his moustache, white from the frothy Guinness which he enjoyed with his Christmas meal. My grandfather always made a fuss of him when he came to us for Christmas, making sure he was comfortably seated and that his glass was never more than half-empty. He probably gave our guest more whiskey and porter than was good for him. When it was time for George to leave, my grandfather suggested that I should walk home with him, as his speech was slurred and his movement unsteady. However, the offer was spurned with more than a hint of righteous indignation.

As soon as he left, my grandfather instructed me to follow him discreetly from a distance in case any harm fell on him. I watched him staggering home, mightily relieved that there was no car on the road for those minutes. I stood outside, my teeth chattering with the cold because I had not taken the time to put on my old grey overcoat, a hand-me-down from a cousin in Galway. I waited for him to turn on his recently acquired electric light and to see him drawing his curtains as he sang, hopelessly out of key, what I think was meant to be 'The Lass of Aughrim'. In truth it could just as easily have been 'White Christmas' or 'Danny Boy'. I waited until I heard no sound, at which time I visualised him sitting down in front of the open fire and falling asleep on the armchair.

I was to recall that night on New Year's Eve, 1981, the night when Ireland was struck by the worst snow blizzard in my memory. The country came to a standstill with drifts of snow. On that night George had what was believed to be a massive heart attack and fell into the open fire, causing the house to go up in flames. By the time the alarm was raised the house was destroyed. The ambulance and the fire brigade came as quickly as the snow allowed. When the fire was extinguished, the badly-charred corpse lay covered in a blanket of snow. The snow seemed somehow appropriate for such an innocent man.

Yes he knows it's Christmas

When I heard the news that shocked the nation before Christmas 2014 that Jonathan Corrie had died homeless on the streets of Dublin, I thought of George and all those like him, who dread the prospect of Christmas and feel that for them there is no room in the inn. I wanted to do something for those that Mother Teresa memorably described as 'the least, the last and the lost'. That is how the idea for this book was born. The question that immediately presented itself was: which cause will I support? An answer quickly arrived in the form of the Peter McVerry Trust, as for as long as I can remember I have admired Fr Peter as the embodiment of all that is best in Christianity in Ireland, because he is someone who walks the walk.

All royalties from this book will go to his Trust. I hope you will enjoy it.

NASTY NICK

Once upon a time there lived a man named Nicholas. He was a tall, thin man with long hands. He always seemed to wear an ill-fitting black suit with an old sky-blue scarf draped around his neck. His once-dark hair was slightly silver now, but the cold blue eyes, set in a craggy face and fringed with the blackest lashes, were the same as when he was a teenager. He had a habit of looking deep into other people's eyes and then into some unseen place. He always said what he thought, sometimes with disastrous results.

Nicholas lived in a lonely house on the side of a mountain by a rutted grass track which led to the tiny village of Whitepark. His house was cheaply furnished. The congealed grease of dinner stuck to plates in his kitchen sink and the porridge dish from breakfast was left drying on the draining board. In the corner of the kitchen was a washstand with a soap dish, basin and a pitcher jug so topped up with water that a fly could drink out of it.

He was the best shoemaker in all the land. People came from far and near to have their shoes made by him. The king always wore shoes carefully crafted by Nicholas' magic hands.

But Nicholas was a sad and bitter man. On Christmas Eve ten years previously his beloved wife had died in a boating accident. It was the end of his world. A sketch of his wife was displayed religiously on his mantelpiece. It whispered to him the secrets of loss and heartache. He felt like a stone had crushed his heart.

Although he had a special talent, Nicholas was not a little feared because of his fierce temper and his rough manner with people. The nickname his neighbours gave him was Nasty Nick, though no one would dare call him that to his face.

The weeks before Christmas were always his busiest time of the year. As the winter dawned, with the rain coming through the holes in the roof and the wind howling through the many gaps in the walls, he needed money badly. He worked eighteen hours a day, seven days a week, because he had a big contract to make new boots for all the soldiers in the king's army.

One evening, six weeks before Christmas, he had a visitor. She had curly, white hair, a very cross face, brown eyes and a false smile. She was a doctor's daughter and that most reviled of species in the locality, a 'blow-in'. No humility and precious little humanity could be diagnosed in her as she looked down her nose in a conscious display of superiority while she spoke to her neighbours. Nicholas eyed her with disfavour when she came into his home. In a voice much too loud for his liking she introduced herself.

'My name is Mrs Frida Fruitcake. You've probably heard of me. My husband, Freddie, owns the biggest bakery in the town. We were featured in *Goodbye* magazine last month. You *must* know of us.'

In an increasingly cross voice, Nasty Nick answered.

'Madam, I've never heard of *Goodbye* magazine. It seems to me that you are a fruitcake by name and nature. I can't afford to waste my time listening to an old bore like you talking rubbish. What do you want?'

Mrs Fruitcake didn't really notice just how angry Nasty Nick was and continued excitedly.

'My darling Freddie has been working hard all year. I would be obliged if you would make him a nice snug pair of slippers for Christmas. They would be lovely for him on the cold nights. I'd pay you handsomely of course.'

Nasty Nick shouted at her in a voice as loud as thunder.

'Do you think I can afford the time to make silly slippers for a man with such a stupid wife? Have you any idea how many pairs of boots I have to make for the king's army? How dare you waste my time? Get out of my sight at once!'

Mrs Fruitcake was so terrified by Nasty Nick's outburst that she began to sob like a baby. She raced out the door faster than an Olympic runner. Nasty Nick followed her out and slammed the door after her so hard that the hinges nearly came off it. He got back to work, muttering under his breath about the stupid woman with the stupid name.

Suddenly he stopped in his tracks. He heard a faint knock on his front door. He scratched his head. Then there was a slightly louder knock on the door. Nasty Nick was fuming.

'Come in,' he said in a very angry voice, thinking to himself that if it was the Fruitcake woman again, he would kill her.

A small, slim woman walked in. She had a small nose and shiny, black hair touching her shoulders. By her side was a little boy.

'Good evening sir,' the woman said in a soft, sweet voice. 'I know you are a very busy man and I'm really sorry to bother you. My name is Lucy Lionheart …'

Nasty Nick gruffly butted in. 'Are you anything to the late Captain Lennie Lionheart?' he enquired.

For a moment it looked as if the woman was about to burst into tears. Then she took a deep breath and said in a whisper, 'He was my husband.'

Nasty Nick shook his head. 'I'm sorry for your loss. I was saddened by the news of his death in the great war seven years ago. People say he was the bravest soldier ever to wear the king's uniform.'

Lucy smiled weakly. 'It is kind of you to say that, sir. My son Lennie here wasn't even born before his father died. I've found it very hard to put food on the table for little Lennie since, but now I've taken on a second cleaning job and at last I can afford to buy some nice things for him. I'd really like you to make him a new pair of shoes for Christmas. The poor boy has never ...'

Nasty Nick stood up from his chair and waved his hands as if he was holding a hot coal. His voice was like a growling dog.

'Madam, do you have any idea who you are talking to or what you ask? Do you think I can afford the time to make silly shoes for a little boy? Have you any idea how many pairs of boots I have to make for the king's army? How dare you waste my time? Get out of my sight at once.'

Mrs Lionheart nearly jumped out of her skin with fear. Her face was white and she fought vainly to hold back the tears. She struggled to keep calm as she said: 'I'm sorry for bothering you. I won't ever trouble you again. Come with me little Lennie.'

Lucy walked to the door. Little Lennie kept looking back over his shoulder as he almost ran with her. Ten years of pain had poisoned Nasty Nick's blood and hardened his heart – but there was something about that little boy's sweet innocent face that touched him deeply inside, and he had never seen such a beautiful woman as the fair Lucy. He felt bad because he had been so horrible to this beautiful woman and this sweet child. Nevertheless, he was shocked when he heard himself say, 'Stop. Come back.'

Lucy walked back slowly with her son behind her, repeatedly tugging at her coat and whispering ever louder, 'Mama no. Mama no. Mama, let's get out of here. Let's get out of here, Mama.'

A look of terror came in his eyes when Nasty Nick walked over to him and raised his hand. Little Lennie almost wet himself as he looked up at this giant of a man. The shoemaker nearly smiled as he said, 'Relax boy – I don't eat children. Wait a second. I'm not promising anything mind, but maybe I might be able to do something. Little boy, let me have a quick look at you again. Oh stop crying. Okay, call back to me Wednesday evening at seven and we'll see.'

Lucy took her son away, not really understanding why Nasty Nick had changed his mind.

'Drat it. Why didn't I just send them packing, especially as I hate Christmas,' thought Nasty Nick to himself as soon as the door was closed. All the same, there was something about that little boy.

He went into the kitchen, picked up an old piece of paper and started scribbling furiously on it. In spite of himself a small smile crept over his face when he saw the finished design for little Lennie's new shoes.

The next Wednesday evening, Lennie didn't want to go back to Nasty Nick because he was so scared of him, but his mother made him. The shoemaker had his measuring tape ready when they called. He looked quickly at the boy's boots with an expert eye. When he spoke, he did so in a surprisingly soft voice.

'Little Lennie, I want to see you here every Wednesday evening for a fitting 'til Christmas Day and on Christmas morning you will call here on the way to church to collect your shiny shoes.'

Each Wednesday the fair Lucy and her son faithfully visited Nasty Nick and on each visit little Lennie's eyes grew wider as he saw new shoes taking shape. Although he never said much to

Nasty Nick, little Lennie began to like the shoemaker, and for his part the shoemaker started to look forward to their visits. As the weeks passed, the visits got longer and longer as the fair Lucy got to know Nasty Nick much better.

Two days before Christmas they had the final fitting. For the first time in ten years the shoemaker had made a huge effort to make his home ready for Christmas. When the knock came on his door on Christmas morning, he raced to answer it. Nicholas was almost dancing with excitement and anticipation. The butterflies were going like mad in his stomach. He opened the door and walked back visibly shocked. For a moment it looked like he had lost his voice. Finally, in squeaky speech, he said, 'Please forgive my manners. Come in. I was expecting somebody else.'

As a group of carollers walked in Nicholas said, 'I would be honoured if you would sing for me. Please.'

After they sang a beautiful version of 'Silent Night' Nasty Nick said, 'My, that was wonderful. Hang on a second.'

He went back into his kitchen and started rooting in one of the cupboards. He came back with a fistful of coins and handed them to the oldest man in the group. The man's mouth opened with surprise.

'But Nasty Nick ... I mean Nicholas, you've become so generous.'

As the carollers left, Lucy and little Lennie walked in. Nasty Nick was smiling like a child in a sweet shop as he greeted his two visitors.

'Well at last the big day has arrived. Oh, happy Christmas by the way.'

Lucy answered with an even bigger smile. 'Happy Christmas.'

Nasty Nick presented the new shoes. Lennie grabbed them and proudly displayed them to his mother, before trying them on.

'Oh little Lennie they're perfect. You've done an amazing job Nicholas. Thank you so much. 'I've never seen anything so lovely. It must be the eighth wonder of the world!' said Mrs Lionheart with awe in her voice.

Nasty Nick made a little bow and said, 'It was my great pleasure.'

Lucy winked up at him. 'Little Lennie has something for you. It's not much.'

Lennie handed the big man a beautifully wrapped parcel.

'Happy Christmas Nicholas. Mama made them for you.'

Nick opened the Christmas paper and pulled out a pair of woollen gloves and a woollen cap with 'Nicholas' written on it, as well as a Christmas card. He turned and wiped away the tears that were toppling in steady streams down his cheeks. Then he said in a choking voice, 'It's been ten years since anyone gave me a present. Thank you so much little Lennie and you too, Lucy. For too long I have lived in the past with all my sadness and anger. You have reminded me that the greatest Christmas gift of all is the present. From now on I will live each precious day as if it was my last. For the first time since my wife died I've had a happy Christmas. I've discovered again that life is a time of mystery, magic, hope and, above all, innocence. It's all thanks to you both. I'm so grateful.'

He quickly took two boxes from under the Christmas tree and presented one to each of his guests.

Lucy's voice was a mixture of surprise and delight as she said, 'Oh Nicholas, you shouldn't have. You're much too generous. We'll save them for later. We must rush now I'm afraid because we're going to be late for church. Nicholas, thank you for all you have done for little Lennie, for both of us. Have a great Christmas.'

Little Lennie chirped in, 'Bye Nicholas. Thanks.'

There was sadness in his voice as Nick said, 'Happy Christmas.'

Lucy and her son rushed for the door. Just as they were about to go out Nick shouted, 'Stop! Lucy there's something I have to say to you.'

The small woman walked towards the big man with a puzzled expression. Lennie followed behind. Nick took Lucy's hand and said, 'You are the fairest of all God's creatures. Make me the happiest man alive and be my wife.'

Lucy almost staggered with confusion. For a few moments the only sound that was heard was the ticking of the grandfather clock.

Then Lennie butted in.

'Oh Mama, say yes. You love him and he clearly loves you. What could be simpler? Say yes and make the three of us very happy.'

His mother turned first to the boy. 'Oh Lennie, are you sure about this?'

Lennie said, 'I've never been more certain of anything in my life.'

His mother smiled shyly as she said, 'Nicholas, I would be honoured to be your wife.'

The big shoemaker got down on his knee, pulled out a ring from his pocket and put it on Lucy's finger.

'Wear this always and know that I will love you forever.'

His wife-to-be said, 'I will always love you Nicholas.'

All three exchanged hugs. Nick looked up to the sky and smiled. 'I'm the luckiest man in the whole wide world.'

As the bells boomed out from the village church Lucy said breathlessly, 'Oh my gosh. Look at the time! We are going to be late for church – but in the circumstances I think God will understand. Nicholas, why not come with us and join us after for Christmas dinner? It's very simple but …'

Nick stopped her. 'There's no meal I'd enjoy more nor no place I'd rather be.'

Nick took both Lucy and little Lennie by the hand and they walked out. Three weeks later Nasty Nick and the fair Lucy got married. Little Lennie was both the pageboy and the best man.

The next Christmas morning a taller Lennie was back in church, but this time he was accompanied by his new twin sisters, Rachel and Ruth. To mark the occasion his stepfather presented a gift to every child in the district. The next Christmas Nicholas presented a gift to every child in the whole country. The following year he donated a gift to children everywhere. Gradually he became even more famous for his love of children than for his wonderful skills as a shoemaker.

Within a few years everyone forgot that his nickname was once Nasty Nick and soon he became known far and wide by his new nickname, Saint Nicholas.

AUDREY'S SIMPLE TRUTH

It was Christmas Eve and Audrey knelt down at the side of her bed to say her prayers. After she said her normal prayers, she added one of her own: 'Please God, make Christmas come for Daddy this year.'

Audrey was eight years old. She loved her father very much, because he was such a good man. However, she found it very sad that he refused to believe in Christmas. He was a very successful businessman who treated all those who worked for him very well indeed. He was used to dealing with money and things he could buy and sell. He had no faith in all that nonsense which Christians celebrate at Christmas: the idea of God becoming human was too far-fetched to be seriously considered by any right-minded person.

He was also very kind and gentle. One day he brought her for a walk in the country. Suddenly Audrey shouted, 'Daddy, Daddy, stop! Stop! There's a kitten back there on the side of the road!'

Audrey's dad said, 'So there's a kitten on the side of the road. We're out for a walk.'

'But, Daddy, you must stop and pick it up.'

'I don't have to stop and pick it up.'

'But if you don't it will die.'

'Well, then it will have to die. We don't have room for another animal. We already have a dog at our house and a cow in our barn. No more animals.'

'But, Daddy, are you just going to let it die?'

'Be quiet, Audrey. We're just going to have a nice walk.'

'I never thought my Daddy would be so mean and cruel as to let a kitten die.'

At that moment Audrey's dad turned around, returned to the spot at the side of the road and bent down to pick up the kitten. The poor creature was just skin and bones, but when Audrey's dad reached down to pick it up, with its last energy the kitten bared his teeth and claws. 'Ssst! Sssst!' said the cat. Audrey's father picked up the kitten, brought it back to the car and said 'Audrey, don't touch, it's probably full of disease.'

When they got home they gave the kitten several baths and plenty of milk.

'Can we let it stay in the house just tonight?' Audrey begged. 'Tomorrow we'll fix a place in the shed.'

'Okay,' her father said.

Audrey watched quietly in the corner as her father fixed a comfortable bed, fit for a prince.

She called their new pet Rex. She loved Rex but her father didn't. Several weeks passed. Then one day her father walked in to the house and felt something rub against his leg. He looked down and there was Rex. He reached down toward Rex, carefully checking to see that Audrey wasn't watching. When Rex saw his hand, it did not bare its claws and hiss. Instead it began to lick his fingers. From that day on he became every bit as fond of Rex as Audrey.

One cold winter's morning he had thrown his coat just inside the door of his shoe shop. When he went back for the coat that evening, Rex had snuggled up inside the coat and was now fast asleep. Audrey's dad did not want to wake the kitten up, so he got a scissors and softly cut the piece off his coat that the kitten was sleeping in and went out in the cold night air with a big hole in his coat.

Most times Audrey's dad was not angry when Audrey did something wrong. One morning he walked into the bathroom and saw Audrey with her face covered in shaving foam and big blobs of cream dripping onto her flowery dress, like a snowman melting in the great heat of the sun.

'Audrey, what are you doing?' he asked.

'I'm saving,' said Audrey.

'You're what?' asked her father, not knowing what she was talking about.

'Saving. Like I saw you doing yesterday morning,' said Audrey.

'Oh, you mean shaving. What do you want to shave for?' asked her dad.

'I want to have a big white beard like Santa Claus,' said Audrey sweetly.

'I see. But you know if you want to look like Santa Claus you need to have a big tummy. Why don't you start by coming down to breakfast with me and letting me fatten you up. We'll have to clean you up first though and clear up all this mess,' said her dad with a big smile on his face.

Audrey's father kissed his wife on the cheek as she headed out to church for the midnight service. As she drove off in the car, snowflakes began to fall, timidly at first, then gathering momentum as the shyness appeared to wear off them.

At that moment, he heard a strange sound coming from the side of the house. Three little birds had been frightened by the sudden heavy snowfall and in their panic had sought to find shelter by flying through the sitting room window. It wouldn't be right to leave these poor little creatures out in the freezing cold, he thought. He decided that he would put them into the bicycle

shed at the bottom of the garden, where they would be dry and
warm. He put on his coat and his big boots and marched through
the deafening snow to the shed. He opened the door wide and
turned on the light. But he could not persuade them to come
into the shed.

Then he got a brainwave. Food will tempt them in, he thought. He rushed back to the house, stumbling a few times on the way in the blanket of snow. In the kitchen he got a few slices of bread and chopped them up into tiny pieces, which he sprinkled on the snow to make a trail into the barn. However, the birds paid no attention to the crumbs and remained in the exact same spot. He tried to direct them into the shed by walking around and waving his arms and shouting at the top of his voice. They scattered in every direction except into the lighted shed. 'They must find me a weird and frightening creature; there is no way I can make them trust me,' he said to himself. 'If only I could become a bird myself for a few minutes, then I could lead them to safety.'

At that very moment, the church bells began ringing. He raised up his hands to heaven. 'Now I know why,' he whispered. 'Now I realise why You had to do it.'

The following morning, Audrey listened attentively as the preacher gave his Christmas sermon. He said: 'The simple truth of Christmas is that God sent his only son to become human like us, so that we might be saved.' Audrey looked up at her father who was sitting beside her. He winked back at her. Audrey smiled to herself and thanked God for answering her Christmas prayer.

TWO LITTLE BOYS

It was the day we got our Christmas holidays from primary school. During the last few days at school before the Christmas holidays, our normal timetable of Maths, Irish, English, History and Geography was suspended. A lot of new Christmas carols were learned. As I had not been blessed with a singing voice and because I felt at the time that singing carols was not an appropriate pastime for an aspiring footballer, I found the repeated singing of these songs nothing less than an endurance test. However, there were lines from individual carols which penetrated my brain, highlighting the catechetical value of these songs. The line that struck me most forcibly was one from 'The Little Drummer Boy': ' … and he smiled at me.' The idea that Jesus was smiling at me stressed my dignity and value in God's eyes more eloquently than any sermon could have done. It was a warm message.

Two lines from 'Little Town' also set me thinking:

> *How silently, how silently,*
> *The wondrous gift is given.*

The image that came to me because of these lyrics was of a shy God; not someone who wanted to be in the limelight, but someone who was more comfortable in the background. Somehow I found that an attractive quality. The mood of 'Joy to the World' was very inspiring and evocative. The picture that came to mind listening to that song was of a dancing God, rejoicing at the happiness of humankind, even if it was only a temporary affair.

Another song we learned was 'Scarlet Ribbons'. In my innocence I presumed this song was a Christmas carol, even though it did not have any apparent reference to Christmas, because it was the story of a little miracle and was designed to illustrate that even a girl's ribbons were a matter of concern in Heaven. My illusions in this respect were rudely shattered when I heard the song on the radio the following summer in the middle of a heatwave.

The miracle these carols celebrated was the making of an all-powerful God, but child-sized, so that even the youngest infant could grasp what it was all about. More importantly, they reminded us of the happy character of our faith, and that Christianity was a reason for rejoicing. God became small for the sole purpose of saving us all. This was part of the beauty of the festive season, where past and future meet in the present.

Learning these carols did have a practical value because we could sing them on Wren Boys' Day. On St Stephen's Day we dressed up in old clothes with blacking and Red Indian-style daubs of lipstick on our faces and cycled to all the houses for miles around, where we sang – or more often wailed – in the confident expectation that we would be rewarded with a few coins for our musical offering. Motley groups appeared on the roads or laneways looking like gangs of tramps in their assorted rags, with faces masked. They did a jig or reel or sang a song, trying to disguise their voices, clinking the coins in their collection tins. Afterwards, they chorused their thanks and went on their way to make more money. Our motivation was purely mercenary, but the carols did help us in a small way to comprehend a mystery we could only dimly understand.

Another important part of our preparation for the season was the making of Christmas cards. Part of this reason was economic: we could give cards to family members and relatives without incurring any expense. There was also a religious reason: at least half our cards had to have a nativity scene drawn on the cover. As a concession, we were also allowed to put non-religious Christmas scenes on some of the cards. However, I suspect the main reason for this activity was that it kept us quiet for hours and hours. There was a bag of sweets for the person with the best card, which provided a definite incentive for us all to do our very best at a time when we were at our most giddy.

That year I also learned my favourite Christmas story. It was the story of how Christmas stopped a war when the fierce and bloody First World War came to a halt on the day of Christ's birth in one corner of the western front. The Germans waved and called out, speaking in simple French; holding out cigars they asked for English jam in return. 'Stille Nacht' and 'Silent Night' rang out on different sides. The words were different but the sentiments remained the same. A football was produced and a game of soccer took place. Music and sport: two of the languages which could have united the participants at the tower of Babel.

The innocence of small children cast a magical spell over our teacher, Mrs Kelly. She had wanted a large family. When pressed further she said she wanted her own football team. But she had no children of her own.

Arguing with her was like going into battle with the sun in your eyes. She could see you coming from every angle and, if a particular ploy was not working, she would smile before you finished the sentence. The smile was the seal of victory. Whenever she was given advice, she had the habit of staying absolutely silent. Then, a few days later, she would thank the person at great length for their excellent advice, only to conclude by saying, 'The pity is I can't remember any of it.'

She was very patient despite the million questions she was bombarded with by me and my classmates. 'Who made God?' 'Where's my teddy?' 'Can we buy ice cream on Sunday?' 'Is Dublin bigger than Australia?' 'How can a man talk inside the radio?' 'How do you spell 'marvellous'?' 'What's the difference between a goose and a gander?'

As I grew older I suspected that she must fantasise about a second home, a tiny cottage by the sea, or even a tree house, where there was room just for her, furnished with a rocking chair, a few books and a radio. No other voices, no other clutter, but space for relaxing and thinking. She must have pined for a little time in the day that was really hers: a little escape which would refresh and rejuvenate her.

No matter what she was always very empathetic. She sensed my low spirits once in December and told me: 'Cheer up. It's not long until Christmas. Do you know what we will do tonight? You can write to Santa Claus and I will post it tomorrow.' My spirits revived immediately. That was her great gift. She always seemed to know exactly what to say to us and when to say it. She always seemed to hit the right note. You could not ask more from a teacher than that.

Some evenings she would put a grain of sugar on our heads so that we would have sweet dreams. Other times she would put a grain of sugar on our eyebrows so that the last thing we would see before we went to sleep and the first thing we would see when we woke up was something nice.

Although she was guilty of overestimating my intelligence, she had some clever educational methods. She used a lot of riddles to make us develop our intellectual powers. Though it was never her intention, she often made me feel a real fool when she caught me out.

'Which is the heaviest – a ton of coal or a ton of feathers?'

'A ton of coal.'

'Are you sure?'

'Ye-e-e-s … I mean no, no' as the penny dropped.

Reading her end-of-year reports was an art form which the KGB's leading expert in cracking codes would find practically impossible to penetrate. It took real skill to disassemble the easy platitudes and decipher their real meaning.

Teachers seldom tell the unvarnished truth about the pupils who are the bane of their lives. There are four principal reasons for their reticence. In ascending order of importance they are: a desire not to hurt anybody's feelings; the law of libel; fear of getting a punch on the nose and the certain knowledge that the parents will wish to extract retribution if any aspersions are cast on their offspring. Hell hath no fury like a parent scorned in full flight at a parent–teacher meeting. Experience teaches teachers that when it comes to writing reports, honesty is not always the best policy.

One of the first skills all new teachers learn from their colleagues is how to pack their school reports with well-worn platitudes. Down through the years, Mrs Kelly had written thousands of such pieces of fiction. In her teacher's code the following dozen comments were endlessly recycled. Each had its own hidden meaning:

1. *A Very Sensitive Pupil.* This student never stops whining.
2. *Dependable in a crisis.* These students take a perverse delight in grassing on their few friends whenever they have done something wrong. They are disliked by students and teacher in equal measure.
3. *Excels at all physical activities.* An out-and-out thug.
4. *Has a very independent mind.* As stubborn as a mule.
5. *His particular gift is for manual activities.* Totally useless at his books.
6. *Expresses herself with great confidence.* Never shuts up.
7. *An exceptionally vivid imagination.* Has an excuse for everything and does nothing.
8. *Works better in small groups.* Can't be trusted on their own for a split second.
9. *A genuinely helpful student.* An insufferable lick.
10. *Requires much praise and encouragement.* A real damning indictment. This student has had an intelligence bypass.
11. *A relaxed disposition.* This is a red-light phrase. These students are bone idle and are as unlikely to pass their exams as Roy Keane is to say something nice about Sir Alex Ferguson.
12. *Steady progress to date.* A sure sign of the teacher's desperation. There is not a single interesting thing that can be said about them. This phrase is only used as a last resort.

My favourite part of each school day was when she read a lovely story. She had a magical way of making the stories come alive. Her stories were the best part of our day, and held our attention more than anything else.

I learned an awful lot about the difference between right and wrong from listening to her stories, especially the one about Ben the Baker. Ben had the nicest bread and cakes in all the land. People came to buy them from miles and miles around. What people didn't know was that Ben was very lazy and never baked anything himself. For years Ben went to bed each night with his bakery empty. Then, while he slept, hundreds of little people from the land of magic came in the middle of the night to bake for him. When Ben woke up in the morning his bakery was full of the nicest cakes you ever saw. He should have been the happiest man alive. But he wasn't. You see, Ben was also very nosy and could not be happy until he found out what happened to his bakery during the night. So, one night, he lit his candle and walked down to the bakery. He could not believe his eyes when he saw all the little people working so hard baking the beautiful cakes. But the little people were scared by the light and the big man with his long beard, so they ran away as fast as they could. And they never, ever came back. The next day when people came to buy their cakes, Ben the Baker's was empty. When word spread around the kingdom nobody ever came to the bakery anymore, and Ben soon had no money.

Mrs Kelly told us that if you must be lazy don't be nosy too! Otherwise you will end up sad and alone like Ben the Baker.

I have to confess that as a little boy some of her comments were wasted on me. A case in point was: 'He-who-lives-in-a-glass-house should never invite he-who-is-without-sin.'

Another of her classics was: 'Politicians are like nappies. Both should be changed regularly and for the same reason.'

Likewise, her puns were wasted on me, such as: 'The nappy market bottoms out.'

Inside the cramped classroom anticipation mingled with apprehension as she stated that she had an announcement for us. A lengthy theatrical pause ensued as she sat in an ordinary armchair which enclosed her like a small cave. Mrs Kelly's statements were sometimes as enigmatic as the Dead Sea Scrolls. A chorus of groans greeted the news that we were to have our annual visit from the community doctor, on this special day of all days. A large frown crossed Mrs Kelly's forehead. Her demeanour was almost always friendly to the point of fervour, but in rare moments, especially if she suspected she was being taken for less than she was, a glacial sternness came over her features and only the resolute hung around to debate. Then her thick-lensed glasses steamed up as she wagged her finger. All thoughts of dissent were suspended and we meekly responded as one: 'Yes Miss.' The width of her smile echoed the generosity of her nature.

Privately we were aghast. Dr Stewart was a short, stocky man whose pugnacious features and brisk, assertive gestures might mark him as a former professional boxer. He usually looked about as cheerful as a man trying to get a cyanide capsule out from behind his teeth. When he formed a set of opinions he was slow to rearrange them. He was to visit us to check our eyesight and hearing.

Almost as one we turned around to look at Stephen. His thin-framed glasses, under high waves of strawberry-blonde hair, partially concealed his shrewd, rather pouchy face. Nonetheless, it was clear that his normally boyishly pleasant expression had been replaced by one of anxiety.

Stephen had been in a car accident six months previously and his face had been disfigured, though the scars were fading. Looking back into the blank spaces of memory, we were unpardonably cruel in the comments we made about him. Stephen's

self-confidence had taken a battering. He also suffered from inter-
mittent hearing loss.

Mrs Kelly decided to give all of our hearing a little test. She
asked us individually to put our right hand up to our right ear
and to repeat back a sentence she dictated to us. There was a
collective intake of breath when it came to Stephen's turn.

Stephen was obsessed with butterflies. The fascination arrived
like talking, too early to remember. I would have bet my last
thrupenny bit that Mrs Kelly would have asked him something
about butterflies – but not for the first time our teacher fanned
the flames of imagination and surprised me.

Stephen's face lightened like a cloudless dawn as he confidently
repeated Mrs Kelly's sentence: 'I wish you were my little boy.'

STRAIGHT FROM THE HEART

The Abbot was distressed. He had woken up that morning early, long before the first faint vestiges of light illuminated the specklings of frost on the hard ground. As he pulled back the curtains, the Abbot was compelled to watch the world take shape, despite his haste. The faint horizontal threads of clouds were growing a fiercer red against the still grey sky. The streaks intensified to scarlet and to orange and to gold, until the whole sky was a breathtaking symphony of colour. Sunrise so rose his spirits that the Abbot could easily understand why dawn worship had been a powerful primitive belief.

In a distant field a proud mother was still licking her newly born calf. A few tattered leaves made a flimsy blanket on the frozen earth. On this day more than any other the monks marvel at the hand of God in the countryside.

By now the monastery was swinging into action. It was a particularly busy day in the monastery as for many it was the time for the obligatory excursion to their Christmas confession, for which they queued interminably.

Tradition in the monastery also dictated that the day before Christmas Eve a great clean-up began and every room in the monastery was turned upside down and inside out as if very special visitors were coming. Everything was dusted, swept, scrubbed, scoured or polished, curtains were washed, and great piles of sticks were chopped and stored in the shed.

The Abbot had always loved Christmas, but this year was going to be a problem because he was going to have to hurt one of his monk's feelings. Some old customs could momentarily transfigure our existence and let the eternal shine through. One such custom was the singing of carols. They struck the Abbot as simple ways of expressing those parts of Christianity that ordinary people found most interesting, not the parts that people ought to find most interesting. They were memorable because they were so tangible. They celebrated things that we could touch and see and warm to: a mother and a baby (though curiously not a father, or at least not a real father), a stable, donkeys, shepherds, straw and hay. Now though, the singing of Christmas carols was causing him a major headache.

The problem had been dragging on for a number of years. All the monks were getting old and although they were still able to do their chores, their voices were well past their best and the community singing had suffered terribly. The main problem was of course Br Noel, who sang, if such a word could be used, in a high-pitched squeaky voice, doing violence to the ears of those unlucky enough to be in his immediate vicinity. Then, one day, as if by a miracle, a young man joined the community who had the voice of an angel. When he sang solo, everyone was enthralled by the sheer beauty of his voice. Time just seemed to stand still. His solo singing brought a dramatic improvement to community worship – but not even he could cover up for Br Noel.

Now the Abbot faced a new problem. The head of the Order

worldwide, Fr Ocome Emmanuel, had unexpectedly sent a message to say he would be starting a three-day visit to the community over Christmas. How could the Abbot possibly subject Fr Ocome to Br Noel's singing? There was only one course of action, the Abbot decided: to instruct Br Noel not to sing while Fr Ocome was visiting. The Abbot didn't want to hurt Br Noel's feelings, but pleasing Fr Ocome was more important than the pride of a simple monk.

Before Midnight Mass on Christmas Eve the Abbot went out for a walk to clear his head and compose his thoughts for his sermon. Having Fr Ocome attend added to the enormity of the occasion. He wriggled his toes and rubbed his gloveless hands to keep warm in the cold of early night. The stars were like holes in God's carpet which allowed the eternal light to shine through. He tiptoed in his shiny wellingtons, avoiding heaps of cow dung in the stable. A hoarfrost lay on the fields and the hedgerows were hung with the lace trimmings of what seemed to be a thousand spiders' webs. The monks' cattle were huddling under creeping hedges, staring vacantly up at the slate-grey sky with their stoic eyes as they churned the day's grass.

When he went back inside a pang of guilt came back to him when he saw poor Br Noel sitting quietly in the back of the chapel. Once Mass started though his conscience eased, as the singing went beautifully.

Fr Ocome was loud in his praise of the quality of the singing. The Abbot went to bed a happy man that night. He smiled contentedly, thinking that the day couldn't have gone any better. He allowed himself to think about the next day and he licked his lips thinking about the feast tomorrow. The later morning hours would run on to the day's highlight, Christmas dinner, roast goose with ham and potato stuffing. The dessert was to be Christmas pudding, boiled in liquid blue flames from a tablespoonful of brandy heated over a candle, and mince pies.

But that night an angel came to visit the Abbot.

'What happened to the singing tonight? We didn't enjoy it as much as usual. We particularly missed Br Noel's singing. He sings the Lord's praises so beautifully.'

The Abbot couldn't believe his ears.

'Br Noel is a terrible singer. He has a voice like a growling dog. How could you possibly enjoy his singing?'

'Ah, you don't understand,' said the angel, 'You see in Heaven, we don't listen to the voice; we listen to the heart.'

THE SHOPKEEPER TURNED
SANTA

Nigel was ten years old and he really wanted a white Christmas, for his mother's sake as much as his own. They had never seen a white Christmas. In fact, the season of goodwill had only ever brought heavy showers of icy rain, which were swept over their village by gusts of bitter wind. The days had been dark and dreary.

His mother would have been a brilliant teacher. Although she generally told the standard children's stories like Little Red Riding Hood and The Five Pigs, there were times when she was more ambitious and went for stories with a little moral. Nigel's favourite was the one about the Indian who was wounded by a poisoned arrow. Instead of pulling it from his side without delay, he spent his time wondering who shot it at him, what sort of feathers were on the flights, and what type of wood the arrow had been made from. While he wasted all his precious time wondering about these trivial questions, the poison was spreading through his body.

Such was the power of her narratives that they touched Nigel on the sensory level. He was enchanted by the scent of the pine air in the mountain freshness of the breeze. His brows almost salted with sweat under the glare of the afternoon sun when she spoke about the summer.

Nigel was the biggest Arsenal fan in history. He had washed cars all summer to buy himself a new Arsenal jersey. It was his pride and joy. Nigel noticed that his mother was looking very sad and tired. He decided he would buy her something nice for Christmas to cheer her up. The problem was that he had no money. The day before Christmas Eve, he decided to go to Mr Hogan's second-hand shop and sell his Arsenal jersey. Mr Hogan explained he didn't sell second-hand clothes, but when Nigel told him the reason he agreed to make an exception. As Mr Hogan was a kind man he paid Nigel a high price for it. The innocence of small children cast a magical spell over Mr Hogan, who had always wanted a family of his own.

Nigel rushed out to the clothes shop nearby and bought a beautiful new blouse for his mother. Her greatest treasure was a silver locket his father had bought for her a few weeks before he died, but she was too poor to afford a new blouse to show it off properly.

The next evening Mr Hogan was shocked to find Nigel's mother walking into the shop. She wanted to sell her locket. Mr Hogan refused to take it at first, but then she explained that she needed the money to buy a pair of Arsenal shorts for Nigel so that he would have the full team strip. Mr Hogan shook his head sadly after his happy customer had left.

After he left the chapel on Christmas Day snow fell softly on Mr Hogan's car. Wind moaned on the telephone wires passing over his house as he went home to an empty house. By then the snow clouds had come in from the west and before he knew it he was enveloped in a blizzard. He noticed a frozen cat outside his garage who wanted to take shelter, like a flock of sheep, behind some wall. Mr Hogan answered her plea; he would not allow the cat to be exiled by the snow. Instead, he took her up in his arms as if she was a precious jewel and ploughed an uneven furrow as he walked through the snow. Once they got in to the shelter and warmth of his kitchen, he placed the cat near his heater and gave her a huge plate of milk.

Mr Hogan had never married and was always lonely on Christmas Day. He was the worst cook in the world and made such a mess of roasting his turkey that he had to throw the badly burnt animal into the bin. His Christmas dinner was a cheese sandwich and a few mince pies.

As he drove later that afternoon to Nigel's house night had fallen early, but the shroud of snow reflected a light that gave eerie life to hedges and house, and by a celestial miracle night was transformed into day. Only the purring car engine shattered the spell of silence. When he got to Nigel's house he plodded up the pathway through the thickening snowstorm, leaving big, deep footprints in the fresh snow. The trees seemed to be standing and shivering together, hugging bare limbs and grumbling about the cold.

Excitement was written all over Nigel's face when he went inside. He was making plans for a monstrous snowman he would build the following day, as he gazed dreamily at the lively flames licking the edges of the turf.

Mr Hogan handed Nigel back his jersey and his mother her locket and a basket of chocolate and biscuits. Their eyes nearly burst with the shock. Nigel's mother said to their guest:

> *As the flowers are all made sweeter,*
> *By the sunshine and the dew,*
> *So this world is made brighter*
> *By people like you.*

'Christmas without kind people like you would be like letters without poetry; thought without imagination or flowers without perfume. Happiness comes to those who cherish others. There is no life without love.'

Mr Hogan replied: 'None worth having anyway.'

Nigel's mum insisted on cooking Mr Hogan a delicious hot meal.

'This is going to be the best meal ever,' said Mr Hogan, with a big smile on his face, as he warmed himself beside a blazing log fire.

'Why do you say that?' asked Nigel in a curious voice.

'I have something up my sleeve,' replied their guest.

'Really. What exactly?' asked Nigel, getting very excited.

'My arm!' said Mr Hogan. He began to roar laughing.

He had the most wonderful laugh in all the land. When he laughed his entire body shook and his tummy went up and down like a yo-yo. His laugh made everyone laugh, and when they laughed that made him laugh again, only louder and longer. Tears of joy rolled down his face.

As he gave both Nigel and his mother a big hug Mr Hogan's final words were:

This Christmas may you both have
Joy enough to share with the world
Peace enough to calm the world
Love enough to light the world.

A CHRISTMAS MIRACLE

A small village in the west of Ireland had a custom where every-one contributed something to the decoration of the Christmas crib. Some brought tiny tinsel stars, a few brought figures of oxen and ass and sheep, and others brought armfuls of straw.

Those who understood woodwork gave their services in helping to build the crib, and the painters of the village were glad to bring their brushes, and to paint on the grand canvas screens erected around the crib the same outdoor scenes that surrounded the stable at Bethlehem.

But the majority of the villagers contributed plants and flowers. For months before Christmas, they pruned, watered and tended to the loveliest of the winter flowering plants, so that they would have something to offer the Holy Child on Christmas morning.

In the town there lived a boy called Harry Minogue. It was always Harry's ambition to contribute something to the crib.

The problem was that his father was a poor man and could not afford to buy anything like the presents the rich women of the parish had bought to mark the birth of this special child. But Harry did not worry. Young though he was, he knew that it was not the value of the gift that mattered, but the spirit in which it was given.

He went into the woods and saw a tiny holly plant and dug it up with his hands. It was a poor little thing without a single berry on it, but Harry carried the offering to the crib on Christmas morning.

When he walked with his offering into the church, the priest placed his little plant right beside the manger in which the baby Jesus lay on a truss of straw.

The place of honour was usually given to the most glowing and colourful plant received, and there were mutterings from those who had given rare and beautiful flowers when they saw that their lovely offerings had been ousted by a poor little colourless holly tree.

'It's a scandal!' said one.

'It defaces the crib,' said another.

'It should be thrown on the rubbish dump,' muttered a third.

Some people started laughing at his miserable-looking plant.

Harry's eyes filled with tears when he heard them making little of his gift. He knelt down before the baby's crib and, in a shaking voice, he said: 'Dear little child, I'm sorry I could not give a beautiful present. The little holly plant was the best I could find, and I give it to you. I always give of my best.'

As soon as Harry had finished speaking a great hush fell upon the stable, for a wonderful thing had happened before their eyes. The colourless little holly plant had become covered with a mass of glowing red berries.

Everybody dropped on their knees beside Harry and prayed like they had never prayed before.

Then the rich women kissed Harry on the cheeks and sent him home. As he left one said, 'Go home my child and remember what you have seen here. Never forget that when you give something with a good heart, God will accept your gift gladly, and, no matter how poor it may be, the touch of His hand will enrich it and make it beautiful.'

THE PIANO MAN

It was the biggest news ever in our parish. We were not just to get a mere parish priest – we were to get a canon. A priest was one thing, but a canon was the ultimate in ecclesiastical and social grandeur. People spoke about the canon's soutane, with the red buttons down the front and silky red satin peering demurely from under the flaps. Others remarked about the delightful swish of a resplendent red monsignorial cassock. The cynics said it was the ultimate clerical status symbol for those who knew deep down that they would never rise to the elevated status of a bishop.

Everyone seemed to be talking about the great honour for the parish to have a canon. In truth no one knew exactly what the difference was between a canon and a parish priest. There were some more sceptical voices that read all kinds of Machiavellian schemes behind this honour. These plots ranged from a shrewd ploy on the part of the bishop to raise more money from the Sunday collection, to a plot to bring the church back to its former glories before the aberrations of the Second Vatican Council.

The Canon was an enigma, a fascinating mixture of conservative and liberal, sinner and saint, intellectual and eccentric. With his grey hair, weather-beaten face, commanding presence and enormous eyelashes, he was not a man to take lightly. He ruled the parish with an iron fist, though underneath he had a heart of gold.

He met his match though in Padraig Walsh, who was not known for his work ethic.

'You don't believe in hard work Padraig?' asked the Canon.

Padraig phlegmatically replied, 'Hard work never killed anyone, but why take a chance on being the first!'

The first time the Canon spoke in public at our Mass the atmosphere was electric, like a revivalist meeting with a touch of fanaticism. The congregation had waited for him to come up to the altar like a presidential candidate. As he spoke, all eyes were on him, seemingly transfixed. It appeared that if he had asked us to try walking on water we would have been happy to do so. Initially he was flattered and honoured but absolutely petrified when asked to speak in public. As letting the 'cause' down was anathema to him he went on to the altar, despite his shaking hands and wobbly knees. There was just a slight tremor in his voice as he intoned his opening words. Public speaking was something he never dreamed of as a child.

He had a particular reverence for Benediction. He loved the choir's singing, the air warm and heavy with incense and bodies and the tinkling of a bell. There always seemed to be a chorus of shrouded coughing coming from the pews from nervous parishioners, answering awkwardly to the Canon's promptings. In silence and solemnity he climbed towards the tabernacle. The monstrance glittered like a metallic sun as he moved it in the shape of a cross before a mass of adoring eyes. I marvelled at the altar boys, clad in scarlet and white, as they left the altar in twos in front of the Canon bearing the empty monstrance, the light from the candles dancing daringly on the gold of his cloak.

One of the people who was to benefit most from the Canon's kindness was the late Biddy Black. She was a music teacher in the convent school and the president of the local branch of the ICA. She sat on the front seat at first Mass every Sunday. She was a small, ascetic woman with grey hair and a very big, booming voice. A proud woman, the highlight of her life was when her son Ignatius entered the seminary in Maynooth. When he was ordained a priest seven years later she was walking on air. From that day on when she was talking to any of the neighbours she always prefaced her important comments with: 'As my son the priest says …'

But then came disaster. Ignatius left the priesthood one Christmas Eve. Biddy was distraught. Her world had collapsed overnight. She stopped going out. Although she went to Mass every Sunday, she sneaked in late and sat on the back seat, and she was too embarrassed to go up and receive Holy Communion. She thought everyone in the parish was laughing at her. Her grief went on unabated for weeks. At that point the Canon decided it was time to take decisive action to restore Biddy's pride and morale. It would have to be handled very subtly however, as Biddy would spurn anything which smacked of charity.

Eventually he came up with a master plan, even though it required him to tell a lie, or at the very least bend the truth substantially. He went to Biddy's house on the first of December and confided in her that his lifelong ambition had been to learn to play the piano. He asked her would she be willing to teach him. Every morning right up until Christmas Eve he went up to her house for an hour-long lesson. That morning he declared that he had achieved his life's ambition and that he could now play the piano with ease. He bowed humbly before his host and then blessed her formally as he told her that she was the best teacher ever. Biddy felt twenty feet tall.

At Midnight Mass that evening she took her old place at the front of the church with her renewed gusto. The whole parish could see that her rehabilitation was complete when she received at Mass again. For the first time in almost a year she talked to her neighbours effusively. Now, she began every second sentence with the words: 'As my best pupil the Canon says …'

THE POWER OF LOVE

Although they were brothers, Peter and Paul did not look much alike. However, the tie of common blood was not all that truly linked the two brothers. They both had the same quick appreciation of the black humour of life, the same kindness and sensitivity and a warm affection for all of God's people.

Both brothers lived and worked together on the family farm. Peter was married with five children, but Paul never married. They shared the workload and what they grew equally and they divided their profits in two halves.

One day Paul said to himself: 'You know, it's not fair that we should share the produce equally and all the money too. After all, I'm all by myself. My needs are simple. However, look at my poor brother with a wife and all those kids.' So, in the middle of the night, he took a sack of grain from his barn and sneaked over to the granary behind his brother's house and left it in there.

Meanwhile, unknown to him, Peter was thinking along similar lines. 'You know, it's not right that we should share our farm produce equally. After all, I'm married and I have five fantastic children who will look after me in my old age. But there is my poor brother with no wife nor family to support him when he gets old.' So that same night he took a bag of grain from his granary, crept over the field between their houses and stored it in his brother's barn.

For the next five years, at the same time every night, the two brothers left a sack of grain in each other's granary. They were both very puzzled as to why their supply did not dwindle. Then one Christmas night, Paul left his home twenty minutes later than normal. He had been delayed because his cow had decided to bring her beautiful healthy young calf into the world. The proud mother was still licking her newly born calf. The calf had a red spot on his white face, so in keeping with the season Paul decided to call him Rudolf.

As Paul carried the sack of grain in the black night he bumped into Peter. Each was startled, but then it slowly dawned on them what had been going on for years and they hugged each other.

Suddenly, the dark sky lit up and a voice came booming down from Heaven: 'Here at last is a fitting place where I shall build my temple. For where my children embrace in love, there my presence shall abide for evermore.'

LET THEM KNOW IT'S CHRISTMAS

'This Christmas we're going to do something different for Midnight Mass,' Fr Dan told his congregation on the first Sunday of Advent. His congregation stirred in their seats, their curiosity aroused. 'We're going to have a living crib.' After Mass his announcement provoked intense discussion amongst the faithful. Everybody was looking forward to this novel development.

As the big day approached the locals were puzzled, because nothing new was to be seen in the church. The normal crib was prepared in the normal way and in its regular place by the faithful gang of volunteers. Fr Dan seemed to be spending all his time going around the parish and collecting the names and addresses of all the poor people in the parish.

At Midnight Mass there was a crush of people. The attendance was swelled by immigrants home from Christmas, a welcome respite for families divided by economic necessity. They were happy, though the snow had formed a moist carpet on their hair and hats. The whole sky seemed to be filled with dizzy, dancing snow. Across the fields the houses glittered, the light from their candles like jewelled pinpoints in the darkness. The atmosphere was as Dickensian as Scrooge after the ghosts.

Fr Dan wore his best gold and white embroidered vestments. The pale wax candles on the altar gleamed amid the lilies. The pungent scent of greenery mingled with the waxy smell of burning candles. The final candle in the Advent wreath was lit ceremoniously. Here mystery and ritual met at the point where human understanding failed. So many of Fr Dan's images of Christ were etched in light, the silver of frost and moonlight, the shining Star of Bethlehem guarding the Magi and the radiance of the candles his father lit in all of the windows of the family home.

Then a solo rendering of 'O Holy Night' that was so beautiful it worked a minor miracle and hushed all the coughing and shuffling. On the window ledges, huge, white candles flickered slightly as a draught touched them, then shone as brightly as before. Despite the solemnity, the smell of incense smelled more beautiful than a springtime primrose.

But still there was no sign of the much talked-about living crib. Had Fr Dan forgotten his promise?

After the gospel the priest turned around and picked up a big, tattered cardboard box. He pulled out two posters and brought the first to the normal crib and pasted it on the wall. On the poster were the words 'Dead Crib'. Then he brought the battered box to the other side of the church and pasted the second poster over it. This sheet simply said: 'Living Crib'.

By now the congregation were totally baffled. Some people were wondering if their priest had lost his marbles. Fr Dan walked back onto the altar and in a soft, gentle voice said: 'These hard times have caused Jesus Christ to change his address. This Christmas he is waiting for you at his new home with one of the poor families in our parish. If you want to greet him you will find the address of each of them in the living crib.'

At first there was stunned silence. Then, one of the congregation stood up and picked a piece of paper from the box. And then another. And then another. Suddenly the whole congregation seemed to be gathered around the living crib and taking a piece of paper each from it. Fr Dan smiled to himself.

In the morning, huge quantities of food, clothes, shoes and toys found new homes. Nobody in the parish could remember a happier Christmas.

SUBBING FOR SANTA

I looked like a pregnant kangaroo and I was more scared than Mickey Mouse in a lake of crocodiles.

It was only in my teenage years I discovered that I was exceptionally tall for my age. Rather than boosting my self-confidence, it actually had the opposite effect as my friends constantly told tall jokes. 'What's the weather like up there?' 'His mother said he won't be long.'

I did have the last word when one friend asked me, 'Do you have a problem with low-flying airplanes?' 'No,' I replied, 'not if I keep my legs together.' As a result of all this teasing I began to walk with a stoop. Then some friends started calling me 'the Hunchback'. The worst time, though, was when I heard one of my classmates, Pat, describe me as 'a long streak of misery'.

None of my previous embarrassments could match this one. Walking around with a pillow tucked into the waistband of my trousers was doing more damage to my frayed nerves and rapidly diminishing self-esteem than to my waistline. If the fashion police had spotted the ill-fitting ball of cotton wool that passed for my beard I would have been convicted for life.

Outside, scurrying shoppers like ants at a party, arms laden with gift-wrapped last-minute presents, headed home as the dusk descended. A crisis in the North Pole had forced Santa Claus to cancel his annual Christmas Eve visit to the children's ward in the local hospital. A near-hysterical nurse – skilled in the art of moral blackmail – had bullied me into taking his place.

The children's ward was transformed. Cards, showing old world people in eighteenth- and nineteenth-century clothes walking about snowy landscapes, decorated the walls. On the top of the tree was a tinfoil star. There were little silver balls, lights like tiny stars and pale-coloured tinsel threaded among the branches. Round the bottom were laid boxes of presents done up in pretty paper and tied with red ribbon.

I hesitatingly took my place in the corner. I'm still not sure why, but there were candles lit behind me. A near tragedy unfolded as I clumsily sat down and my red cloak brushed against one of them. It took a few seconds for me to understand the significance of the little girl screaming, 'Santa's dress is on fire! Santa's dress is on fire!' As soon as I did I found a burst of speed that Ronaldo would have killed for and sprinted to the bathroom with a trail of smoke coming out of my rear end.

I still have nightmares about the sight I saw in the mirror after I had put out the fire. Without a shred of dignity left I made my way back to my seat, a soggy red and white mess. By then all the candles had been quenched.

The children were getting restless. My first customer was a pleasant girl called Simone who gave me the most thorough inspection I've ever been subjected to. I was rather unnerved by her first question: 'Do you know Sarah-Jane-Palmer-Butler?'

I could have kicked myself when I heard myself answering, 'I don't even know half her.' This was no way to make friends with the enemy. I decided to seize the initiative and pull the biggest present I could lay my hands on out of my red bag and handed to her without any further chit-chat. It was some kind of computer game – at least that's what I think it was. Simone was thrilled and I felt the tension suddenly ebb from my body.

To my surprise, I started to enjoy myself as an agent of good cheer. The gifts I handed were examined with squeaks of delight and excitement, though there was the odd face as sad as a flooded lawn if the present did not live up to expectations. New Arsenal kits and One Direction CDs elicited great whelps of joy.

My last client was a little girl who only had one arm. As she unwrapped her present her face creased in wonder. Immediately her face brightened. Her voice was sure with love, and her smile explained the whole meaning of the universe.

Euphoria was too mild a term to describe the elation and exhilaration I felt, scarcely able to contain my joy. No words can adequately convey this feeling. There are moments when it seems the gods are on your side – when nothing can possibly go wrong. A lifetime seemed to be crowded into the space of a second.

Our eyes met and a warmth went through me that I had not felt before. In that moment, I learned the real meaning of the season: the greatest gift at Christmas is giving.

UNTO US A CHILD IS BORN

Once upon a time there lived a girl called Sarah. She was a shy eight-year-old who was unable to see evil in others. Although her nose was a little lumpy, her teeth were crooked and her eyebrows were too dark, she had a real beauty to her. Most days she looked slightly untidy. Her hair was never neat and she generally wore clothes that were either too big or too small for her. Her room was such a mess she had to wipe her shoes *after* leaving it. She sometimes spoke slowly and then used her hands to help find and say the right words. When she listened, she played with her long, jet-black hair and often seemed to be biting a fingernail.

Sarah was a dreamer and usually didn't pay much attention to what she was doing or where she was going. She often got lost on the way to school. Her father said that she had a brain the size of a pea but that her heart was bigger than a horse.

On one particular morning, Sarah was in a state of total panic. Her tummy ached, her head spun around like a demented dragon and her throat felt like it was carrying around broken glass. That morning, she had been carrying home a big bowl of water. It was much too heavy really for an eight-year-old like herself but she always did what she was told. She had almost made it the mile and a half home when she lost her balance and the bowl crashed onto the ground, smashing into a hundred tiny pieces. She knew immediately that this meant big, big trouble from her father.

Sarah's dad had a terrible temper and she hated it when he was in bad mood. Most of the time he was very nice and kind but when he got angry he got really, really angry. And when he was angry he wasn't a pretty sight.

She knew that her dad would not be smiling when he saw the broken bowl. Her late mum had given him that bowl for his birthday and it was something he always treasured. Now Sarah had broken it. Her dad would be so angry and would shout at her very loudly. He was the nicest and most gentle creature you could ever meet. But if he ever lost his temper you didn't want to be near him. It was like watching a volcano explode. You just wanted to get as far away as fast as possible. Heaven help you if you got in his way.

He would be home soon. What, oh what, could she do?

With tears in her eyes, Sarah decided she would run away.

Sarah ran and ran until she got very tired. 'Why do I always make a mess?' she thought to herself. She remembered the last time she had made a mistake. Her aunt Molly was getting married and everybody was in a tizzy. Everyone was given a job to help out. All Sarah had to do was to look after the wedding cake while the rest of the family got ready for the party afterwards.

She went out to play with her friends and forgot about the cake until it started to rain. The rain swept in windy puffs across the fields. As she went home, Sarah started to panic. Her worst fears came true. Her dog, Lassie, was licking the wedding cake.

Lassie was warm, brown and smooth-coated, with a cream arrow on her forehead and flecks of cream on her two front feet. She was a very caring, friendly creature and Sarah loved her with a passion. At that moment, however, Sarah could have killed her dog, as cake-icing dripped from Lassie's whiskers. The damage to the cake was small and Sarah tried to fix it with a knife.

As she cut the cake at the wedding her aunt looked very happy, as if she was the mother of the child who has just won first prize at the pretty baby competition. To Sarah's eyes the icing looked as buttery and soft as white custard, and everyone agreed they had never tasted nicer wedding cake.

Sarah had not got into trouble for the wedding but she knew she would get into big trouble for breaking her father's bowl. She stopped running when she got to her local town.

Bethlehem was normally a quiet place but that night it was full of people. Sarah remembered that it was the time that the government was counting all the people in the country and everybody was filling out lots of forms.

Sarah was frightened by all the activity and started to cry. A kindly old shopkeeper saw her distress and gave her an armful of fruit. Sarah was overjoyed and went to find a quiet place to enjoy this feast.

Just as she was sitting down outside a stable she saw some shadowy figures emerge from the darkness. As she rose to her feet she saw a man helping a very fat woman down off a donkey's back. Although the woman was beautiful, Sarah had never seen anybody looking as tired or dusty. The man looked very thin and hungry.

What upset Sarah the most though was the sound of the woman moaning in pain and holding her stomach. That poor creature must be very hungry, thought Sarah. Instinctively she brought over all the fruit to the couple. They thanked her warmly and then the man helped the woman into the stable and lay her down on a bed of straw. He told Sarah that his name was Joseph and that his wife's name was Mary.

A few minutes later Mary started moaning and screaming loudly. Joseph called out for help. Very quickly a group of men, all with beards and wearing strange clothes, came into the stable to see what was happening.

Sarah sneaked a glance up at them. One of the men saw her and gave her such a fierce look that she fled into the corner like a frightened rabbit. Sarah's fear grew when another man asked her name. She was too scared to say anything. She wanted to answer but her mouth seemed frozen. The man patted her on the head and said: 'Don't be scared. We had our breakfast and we only eat little girls like you on our birthdays.'

Then he laughed. It was a big, booming laugh. Sarah was afraid he would split his sides he was laughing so hard. Then Mary started moaning and screaming again and the men went to help her. There was a lot of noise but Sarah couldn't see what was happening because the men were blocking her view. A few minutes later the men stepped back and Sarah had a big surprise. She saw Mary lying in the corner with a baby in her arms. Except Mary wasn't fat anymore. How could anyone go from fat to thin so quickly? Sarah thought to herself. Sarah could see the baby was a boy. Joseph was crying softly. Sarah had never seen a man cry in front of other people before. Yet he also had a smile on his face. How could anyone be crying and smiling at the one time? This was very strange.

Mary called Sarah over to see the new arrival. Studying the new baby was incredibly exciting. Sarah loved the baby's small, chubby face, with his constantly changing expressions, his tiny hands and fingers swinging around like a bicycle wheel and his round tummy.

Sarah stroked his silky, strawberry blonde hair with great caution, afraid that the baby's head might roll off if she touched him too hard. As she relaxed, she thought that nothing had ever been so soft and fine. The baby's little mischievous smile made Sarah smile. As Sarah was exploring the new baby there was a big discussion going on between Joseph and Mary as to whom the baby looked like.

'He is like his great uncle Albert,' said Mary.

'Not at all. He is not on that side of the family. He is more like his great-grandmother,' replied Joseph.

'I don't think so. He is more like his first cousin Jimmy beside the Red Sea,' said Mary.

'What are you talking about? He is the cut of his grandfather,' answered Joseph.

Sarah went outside to let Joseph and Mary talk in peace. She thought she should get some help so she went in to the chemist shop a few hundred yards away. She walked up to the counter to a man who was holding a jar of medicine in his hand and she told him about Joseph and Mary and their new baby in the stable. But the man was very grumpy and said in an angry voice: 'I don't know what you're telling me for. I only work here.'

Sarah walked sadly back to the stable. Suddenly she remembered her father. She knew that he would be worried about her so she said her goodbyes and began her journey home.

As she started to walk she felt a great sense of peace come over her. Darkness had fallen like an angry giant. On her way she saw a great star in the east. She remembered that her old teacher Mrs Hatchetface had told her that there was a story that a star would come from the East to guide the three wise men in search of a baby who would save the world. The only problem was that they couldn't find three wise men in all the East, so three wise women would come instead.

She was just outside the town of Bethlehem when she saw three beautiful women, with dark skin and wavy hair, in magnificent robes on camels. They were carrying what looked like very expensive presents.

'Young girl do you know where the new king was born tonight?' one asked.

'I'm afraid I know nothing about that ladies but there was a lot going on in Bethlehem this evening,' said Sarah.

'Please tell us what you saw,' said one of the women. 'My name is Ruth, by the way, and this is Roberta and Rachel.'

While Sarah told everything that had happened to her, the three women listened very carefully. When she had finished, Ruth asked, 'I know you are very tired but would you be kind enough to take us to see that woman in the stable?'

'My Dad told me never to talk to strangers, but you seem very nice so I will help you,' replied Sarah.

Quick as a flash, Ruth stretched out her long arm and pulled Sarah up beside her on her camel. The three camels took off at great speed. Sarah was a bit scared but she was also thrilled. It was her first time on a camel. A short time later they reached the stable.

Even before they got to the door Sarah could hear the new baby crying. She saw a few men rushing in before them in a state of great excitement. Some of them were carrying armfuls of clean straw.

Sarah walked in behind the three women and peeped out from behind one of the big men to see Mary holding her new baby. No woman could look happier.

There were a lot of holes in the stable walls, so a chilly wind was blowing through, giving Sarah the shivers. The men were standing with their mouths open and their hands in their pockets. They had no idea what to do.

The three women took control. They told the men to stand back. Ruth pointed to two of the men and in a strong voice said, 'Get that donkey out of here. Can't you see it shouldn't be in the same place as a baby?' The two men did as they were told as if they were little children. Sarah thought Ruth must be a teacher, she was so good at giving orders. The woman told Rachel that her name was Mary and that the man's name was Joseph.

Then the three women presented gifts to Mary. Roberta went first and she gave the new mother a basket of lovely soaps and oils and facecloths, as well as the tiniest clothes Sarah had ever seen. Roberta bathed Mary and her baby with some of them. When Mary and her baby were nice and clean she dressed the baby in some of his new clothes. As it was very cold in the stable she put on the cutest little woollen cap on his head and lovely little gloves on his tiny hands.

Next came Rachel, and she presented Mary with a beautiful silk nightdress and dressing gown. The nightdress had an amazing twirly design and the dressing gown was covered in little stars. Rachel held the baby as Mary put on her new clothes. Sarah thought she looked like a queen. All that was missing was a crown for her head. Rachel then took out a hairbrush and brushed Mary's long, black hair, as if she was preparing her for a big party rather than to sit in a stable.

Last was Ruth, who opened the wrapping paper off a bulky object. Mary's eyes nearly fell out of her head when Ruth calmly put a magnificent crib on the strawy floor and placed the baby in it and wrapped his blanket around him. Finally, Ruth gently left a book beside the baby, who already had the most magical smile. It was a copy of the famous Jewish folk tale – *The All New Adventures of Larry Totter*.

In whispery voices Mary and Joseph thanked the three women for their beautiful presents.

Sarah felt very happy because of all the great things she had seen. On her way home she met her father's friend, Noel. He told her that her dad had gone to the church to pray that she would get home safely because he was worried about her.

By now it was hard to see her way. It was a dark night, as black as the ace of spades.

As she walked, Sarah met a group of shepherds who asked her what had happened in Bethlehem. One shepherd had curly white hair and a very cross face, but the others were shy, kind people so Sarah did not feel afraid of them. She said: 'A child has been born who will turn the world on its head and heal the sick, give sight to the blind, feed the poor and be good to everyone. His love will shine a light into every corner of the world.'

Then one of the shepherds whispered: 'Then it is true. About an hour ago an angel appeared to us as we sat around our campfire. We were tired from looking after our sheep all day and very cold so we had been drinking whiskey to keep us warm. The first thing the angel said was: "Be not afraid." But we were terrified! Really, I mean it. We were sacred out of our wits! We had never seen an angel before. We thought we must have done something very wrong or that we were in trouble for drinking whiskey. We had never looked at an angel nor smelled an angel nor heard an angel's voice. The angel's voice was kind of strange, like nothing we had ever heard before. The smell the angel gave off was so pure it almost hurt our noses. Then the angel said a second time:

"Be not afraid." And once again we were terrified!

'The angel went on to say: "Tonight a child is born who will save the world." Just when we thought things could get no stranger the angel started singing. Over and over again it sang: "Glory to God in the highest and peace to all people on earth. Listen now and hear what I have to say. All children will live for ever more because of Christmas Day."

'The angel told us that we would never feel really bad again and that there would always be a light in our hearts and that we should go and see this new baby by following a star in the East. That's what we tried to do but the star was high in the sky and once it started snowing we couldn't see it anymore and we got lost. Before you came along we were starting to wonder if we had imagined it all, because you never expect you will get a visit from an angel. So we're so glad to have met you and we will go quickly to Bethlehem now to see the new baby. Thanks little girl. Travel safely.'

Sarah said goodbye to the shepherds, who went off to see Joseph, Mary and Baby Jesus at such speed that it was the first Christmas rush! It was only then Sarah understood that she had seen something really extraordinary that night.

When she was near home she saw her dad. When he caught a glimpse of her a huge smile formed on his face.

He rushed up to Sarah and gave her a big hug and what must have been ten thousand kisses. Sarah didn't know if she should laugh or cry. She said in a soft voice: 'I'm really sorry I broke the bowl that Mammy gave you, Daddy. I'm so sorry.'

Her dad laughed. 'Don't worry about the bowl. I can always buy a new one but I can't buy a new girl like you. Relax. Nobody's cross with you. I'm so glad you are home safely.'

Her father was astounded when Sarah told her story of all the wondrous things she had seen. He said: 'You know that in thousands of years children all around the world will be talking about what happened tonight. Shopkeepers will sell cards about it. Gift shops will open to make presents about it. Bakeries will bake cakes to celebrate it. People will wonder about what really happened. But you were there in the stable, my darling. You are so lucky. That is probably the greatest gift anybody could ever get. Everyone who missed tonight in Bethlehem has really missed out. This is the day the Lord has made. You will remember this for the rest of your life and even longer. Tonight's events will echo in eternity.'

HIDDEN TREASURE

The Mother Superior was distraught. Her convent was in a bad way and was literally falling apart, but there was barely enough money to feed her community, let alone for any repairs. All year her fellow nuns had been saying to her, 'We'll have to leave.' The Mother Superior always replied, 'Have no fear. God will provide.' But as the winter advanced, she had a change of heart. To her, it seemed cruel to put her older nuns in particular through such hardship. At the start of Advent, she reluctantly decided that she would close the convent at Christmas, but she decided to keep her intentions a secret.

That night, she had a strange dream. She had a vision of walking to the city and finding a large chest of treasure in the garden with the giant Christmas tree. Each night for the next week she had the same dream.

The Mother Superior was not the sort of woman to believe in foolish dreams, but in her desperation she decided she would walk to the big city to search for the treasure. The long journey took three days. She spent the nights in lonely stables.

If a stable was good enough for the baby Jesus, she thought to herself, it was certainly good enough for her.

Finally, she reached her destination. Somebody pointed her in the direction of the big Christmas tree. Even from the distance she could see that it was exactly like in her dream. A tremor of excitement raced through her body. Maybe her dream would come true after all.

Her joy vanished as she got nearer to the tree. There was no garden – just a big concrete square. She sat on the bench feeling very foolish. Her disappointment became too much and she started to cry. A tall man sat down beside her. He spoke very softly and he was a great listener, so to her surprise the Mother Superior heard herself telling the story. The man said, 'That's very strange. Last night I had a dream that I would discover treasure beside a wishing well.' The nice man insisted on taking the nun into a local inn for a meal. Shortly afterwards, feeling a little more refreshed, she began the long walk home.

Snow was falling lightly when she returned, cold and wet, to the convent late on Christmas morning.

She went straight out into the back garden. 'It couldn't possibly be,' she thought to herself as she looked at the old wishing well in the corner.

To the amazement of her nuns she started digging beside the well. Three hours later, as darkness fell, she had found nothing. The only spot left was under the statue of the baby Jesus. It broke her heart to have to break the statue but she felt she had no other choice. Ten minutes later she shrieked for joy as she opened a huge treasure chest full of gold coins.

The Mother Superior smiled to herself as she said, 'Christmas has come.'

CHRISTMAS GUESTS

Linda Golden's Christmas dinner was a very simple one of eggs, hot cocoa, biscuits and butter.

Tears came to her eyes, not for the first time that day, as she thought of her late husband. How quickly those marvellous years when they were so happily married had melted away.

Linda woke from her afternoon slumber with a start. A crashing sound boomed through the still air. Somebody was knocking at the door. Linda's heartbeat accelerated; nobody ever came here any more, but last night she had the strangest dream that the Lord himself would visit her on his birthday. Linda herself had been born on Christmas day, seventy years ago.

Her face fell when she saw a shabby old beggar standing on the doorstep. What a foolish old woman I am becoming, she thought to herself. The stranger's clothes were ragged and threadbare and his shoes were badly worn out. Linda brought him inside, sat him beside the fire, gave him a mug of steaming tea and went off to look for her late husband's old coat and boots. They fitted the stranger perfectly. With tears in his eyes, the old man bade farewell.

Linda started to tidy up. Within moments, through the clear frosty air, there came a faint knock. This time it was a bent old woman. She had curly white hair, a very haggard face, brown eyes and a sad smile.

'Could you give me some money and God bless you ma'am?'

Linda shook her head regretfully. 'Come in anyway!' The old woman sat beside the fire while Linda made her some hot tomato soup and gave her two slices of brown bread. The woman looked at the 'feast' with delight and savoured every mouthful. Then after a short chat she left, warm and contented.

Linda thought how strange it was that she should be visited by two strangers in such a remote place. An hour and a half later there was another knock. This time it was a beautiful, slim, pale-faced young woman.

'I'm really sorry to trouble you but would you mind if I came in and sat down for a few minutes because I think I have twisted my ankle?' Linda bathed the ankle and bandaged it expertly to prevent any swelling. The young woman thanked her sincerely and Linda walked her to the door and they exchanged goodbyes.

Linda shut the door and went back inside. What an extraordinary Christmas day it had been! She walked over to the mantelpiece and picked up the old book. It was covered in a sheet of dust. After a short search she found the lines she was looking for:

> *For I was a stranger and you gave me welcome,*
> *I was naked and you gave me clothes,*
> *I was hungry and thirsty and you gave me food and drink,*
> *I was in pain and you gave me comfort.*

A sudden twinkle came back into Linda's eyes. Dreams come true after all!

HELMUT'S MEET AND GREET

It was Christmas Eve.

The angel Helmut was the nicest, most generous, most hard-working angel in all of heaven. Like all good angels, Helmut did his best work in the shadows and never sought any reward for his toil. Eventually though, all the other angels asked God to give him a special Christmas present. The angel Gabriel came to Helmut and told him that God would grant him his fondest request on Christmas Day to mark the birth of the Lord. As a deeply spiritual angel, Helmut said: 'All I want is a short private audience with God on Christmas morning.'

When the time came, Helmut entered God's parlour and had a lovely cup of celestial coffee. Then God said: 'My special angel, I know you have something you want to ask me. What is it?'

Helmut had just one question: 'Which is most important: the head or the heart?'

God paused pensively before telling the following story.

❄ ❄ ❄

Head said: 'I am full of bright ideas.'

Heart said: 'I am full of tenderness and passion.'

Head said: 'I am reason. I am order. I am the lynchpin which holds everything together.'

Heart said: 'I am feeling. I am mystery. I am the creative energy which sparks wonder and authentic life.'

Then Head and Heart began to squabble. Head said: 'You are easily swayed and misled. You live in a world without order.'

Heart replied: 'You are dispassionate and detached. You don't live. You just exist.'

So Head and Heart went to God and asked if they could be split up. God laughed at them and said: 'You two belong together. Apart, you are worthless. Head, you are the container. Heart, you are the contents. The container without the contents is as useless as an empty vessel, all sham and no substance. The contents without the container will scatter to the ends of the earth, and blow into the empty wind. It's not possible for you to live apart and have productive lives.'

Head and Heart were puzzled. 'But we are total opposites. How can we find harmony?'

God said: 'Draw close and embrace like lovers. Protect each other. Look out for each other. Help each other to be equal partners. Then you will join together as one and I promise you something fantastic and wonderful will happen this Christmas.'

At this Head and Heart asked in unison: 'What?'

God simply smiled and said: 'Wait and see.'

THE NEW KING

David's Christmas Day began as all his days had begun, meandering through the countryside in search of a breakfast of bountiful blackberries. This was his favourite time of the day, the only pleasure in his poverty-stricken life. Suddenly, he came to an abrupt halt, his attention caught by a wooden notice, written in bold handwriting and hanging precariously on a magnificent oak tree.

It was common knowledge throughout the kingdom that the reigning king had no heir and was frantically searching for a successor, as he was now in his eighty-fifth year. The sign on the tree showed that he was trying for a different approach: now, every qualified young man should apply for an interview with the king. The qualifications were very specific – love of God and love of neighbour.

David thought long and hard about the notice. Even though he was a very modest young man, he considered that he indeed loved God and his fellow human beings. He decided there and then that he would go to be interviewed by the king. However, there were obstacles, which had to be immediately overcome. He was so poor that he had no clothes which would be presentable in the king's palace. Worse still, he had no money to buy the food and clothes he needed.

David's journey was almost complete when he came upon a poor beggar sitting feebly on the side of the road. His haunted eyes, his ashen face, his outstretched arms pleaded for help, much more loudly than any words ever could have.

David's heart was so moved with tender compassion at this picture of vulnerability and suffering that he immediately stripped off his new clothes and swapped them for the beggar's rags. He gave all his food to the beggar without the slightest hesitation. The beggar smiled in grateful appreciation as David headed off uncertainly to the king's castle. David felt completely out of place as he waited, for what seemed like an eternity, to be presented to the king.

When the moment arrived, his heart was in his mouth as he bowed before the king. When he raised his eyes, he was shocked to see the king's face.

'But you … you were the poor beggar by the side of the road.'

'Yes,' answered the king. 'I was that shabby beggar.'

'But, why did you put me through all this?' asked David.

'Because I had to find out if you really do love God and your fellow human beings. I knew that if I came to you as king, you would have been so dazzled by my crown and robes that you would have bent over backwards to do anything I wished, but I would never have known what was really in your heart. So I came to you as a simple beggar, with no claims on you except for the love in your heart. Now I know that you truly do love God and your fellow human beings. You shall be the new king.'

The Ghosts of Christmas Past

The ticking of the small alarm clock, lying downwards on the old Apple Macintosh computer, breaks the stillness of my kitchen. The milk in the jug has gone a bit off in the past day. The mug of steaming tea is strong enough to float my cap on – if I had a cap. I put on my CD of U2's *Joshua Tree* for the ten thousandth time before dipping into the newspaper. Yet another story about the financial crisis; a major movie is to be made in Dublin with a string of top Hollywood names involved, maybe even Robert De Niro; a new clamp down is ordered on urban crime; and a celebrity I have never heard of is spotted with a mystery man in Kerry.

My drowsy eyes suddenly explode into life at the sight of a black-and-white photograph of an old man and a young boy patting a horse. The picture is like a Pandora's box which opens a cascade of emotions within me. Despite my best efforts to the contrary, tears blur my vision and topple in steady streams along my cheeks. In that moment I am transported to another time and place.

Arkle was a wonder horse, and my first hero. I had no idea of my own family tree, but I knew everything about Arkle's. My most enduring memories of my father are of horses on summer days. He would carry a bag with two bottles of tea wrapped in two old stockings as we went off to save the hay. When he took a break for his meal he filled my head with stories of Ireland's greatest racehorses. Just to be in his company made me feel that the world was in season.

I loved going with him to the bog. Although it was back-breaking work, there was something special, almost spiritual, about the bog. The scent of turf fires and bog tea was a sensory pleasure. All human life was there. Women, men, young, old, happy, sad, the industrious and the lethargic. Although it was a very exposed terrain if the weather was nasty, when the sun was shining I always felt that God was smiling on the world. Everything was in harmony. It was my very own Garden of Eden.

Another particularly warm memory for me was the day my father brought home our first television set when I was four.

My happiness was not to last. On the last Saturday in one October of my fifth year on this earth, my father died. He was thirty-five years old. Looking back now, I mourn for the unfinished business between us – so many things that I would have liked to say but never got the chance.

Grandpa

When my father died my grandfather became possibly the most important person in my life. I was called after him. His birthday was even the same as mine.

I loved being with him on the rare occasions when he was working with the horse. I was enthralled by the magnificence of the animal; to me it seemed noble, imperious, majestic, powerful. Yet my abiding image of my grandfather is him in his donkey and cart. The donkey knew the fields so well that there was no need to steer. The only flaw in his make-up was that he had a fear of water, arising from the fact that he had fallen into a bog hole in his youth.

If there was one reason I loved my grandfather so much it was that he always listened to me. He never cut me off in midstream. I always felt that he valued my opinion, even when my ideas were totally hare-brained. I was deeply grateful that he was living with us.

On a Sunday morning sidewalk

Although breakfast on Sunday morning was always conducted in semi-silence in deference to Ciaran MacMathuna, my grandfather's favourite music was birds singing. He especially loved the cuckoo, which sent its voice of mystery from out of the woodland depths and into wide open spaces, calling nature to rejoice at the advent of spring.

The song of the cuckoo was an echo of the halcyon days in paradise, rendering nature what it truly is: beautiful; poetic life at its innocent best; the world as it ought to be; the ideal for a moment realised. As we took refuge in a canopy of trees during April showers, everything seemed made from memory. The sound of the cuckoo enshrouded us with a redemptive feeling, melting away depression, pain and bitter disappointment. Her dulcet tones hinted at a bygone age of innocence and values that could no longer be obtained. The music was sweet and sensual, evocative of a higher world.

From my grandfather's point of view, the most disappointing result of the change of landscape was the virtual disappearance of the corncrake. They were the victims of progress; when silage came in their natural habitat was destroyed. It was my grandfather who first introduced me to the sweet sound of the corncrake. Once we had gone out in the still night to check a newborn calf, we drank together from the bird's symphony of raucous notes pleading in the night. He seemed to invoke not just good tidings, but elation. I always associated that sound with sun-drenched summers in the age of my innocence before my father died.

Memory is blurred and softened by time, but I always remember those summers as times of perpetual sunshine, bright moonscapes and the sound of laughter. I wondered if the corncrake suffered from insomnia – he always seemed to be in full voice just as everyone else was trying to sleep. I often cursed the age of silage for depriving me not just of the corncrake, but of all the nostalgia, wide-eyed simplicity and unadulterated happiness that went with him.

Thou shalt not kill

Some of my friends at school spent their evenings stealing birds' eggs and vandalising nests. My grandfather made me solemnly swear that I would not partake of such activity. He saw it as a crime against nature, as well as psychologically and spiritually unhealthy, claiming: 'Every time we kill something, something inside *us* dies too.'

The countryside smells changed also. I was never crazy about the scent of horse dung, but it was infinitely preferable to the pollution and impregnating smoke of tractors and heavy agricultural machinery. The sweet smell of hay was an almost sinful pleasure. By comparison, the assault on one's nose by silage was vulgar. In the haymaking season it always seemed that all the scents of the earth and growing things which had been imprisoned were released by the summer sunshine in waves of piercing sweetness.

Tastes were changing too. Around this time my sister almost provoked a riot when she announced – to both my grandfather and mother's horror – that she would no longer drink 'cow's milk' or eat homemade butter. When questioned as to where the milk would come from she replied in all sincerity: 'From a bottle in the shop.' I thought it would have been wiser to keep quiet about it, rather than risk starting World War III by asking my mother to do the unthinkable and *buy* butter. My sister, though, had no such scruples. After three tense days a compromise was eventually reached. She agreed to drink cow's milk and my mother agreed to start buying butter.

As I got older, our carefully concealed bottle of poitín became an important feature of my life, particularly during the lambing season. When the lambs were born on cold nights, especially after a difficult birth, they were sometimes close to death and too weak to stand up. One of the most effective ways of pepping up the lamb was a spoonful of poitín. If the night was particularly cold, the semi-comatose lamb was wrapped in an old coat or jumper, then brought into the house and put in a wooden box beside the fire. Such a box was a semi-permanent fixture around all sheep-farming households.

For 'medicinal purposes' my grandfather had a bottle of poitín stashed away in the top of his wardrobe. As poitín was an illegal beverage, it was important that it was kept out of sight. I got into hot water when I was eight years old when I mistook a bottle of poitín for a bottle of holy water and gave it to a distant cousin home from America.

O happy day

My grandfather's favourite time of the year was Christmas. He loved the rituals. There was the obligatory excursion to the friary for Mass, preceded by confession, for which we queued interminably.

That night, too, the goose, which was to form the main course for the Christmas dinner, was plucked and left hanging on the back of the shed door outside. Disaster struck one night when a mini-storm caused the door to open, allowing our two cats to enter. By the following morning, the goose looked rather anaemic. A crisis was averted when a neighbour gave us one of his geese in return for a few bags of turnips. I often wondered if, in the middle of the fourth century when Pope Julius I decided that Christ was born on the 25th of December in the year zero, he could have foreseen the implications of this date for turkeys and geese in the years to come.

The next evening was always the time for setting up the crib. This task was conducted with an air of great solemnity. The shepherds and the angels, the ox and the ass were all carefully wrapped in old newspaper to preserve their bright colours. All this was stored in a box in the loft in the outside shed. A winding staircase led up through what appeared as an extraneous round tower and there was the most fantastic collection of bric-a-brac and memorabilia collected in my grandfather's lifetime.

Simply the best

I knew instinctively that this was a profound event, and so Christmas challenged me to be the best I could be. In the immortal words of Johnny Mathis, a ray of hope was flickering across the sky. A child was being born who would turn the world on its head and heal the sick, feed the poor and bring the world eternal life. Put simply, because God so loved the world he was sending his only son. On that holy night the Word was made flesh. One of the most important truths of the Christian faith which this night embodies is the fact of God's trust in humanity. The Nativity highlights most starkly the full measure of human responsibility and human destiny, as it is a declaration of God's trust in humankind. The unknown God who is Lord of all discloses to people that if they want to know what he is like, they should look in the stable – at a human life.

This baby comes as 'the way, the truth and the life'. He comes to bring 'the Good News to the poor'. It is a particular kind of Good News because its truth hurts as much as it liberates. Sadly, there are many cosy corners that need to be challenged and many aspects of contemporary society that stand in need of liberation. For all our talk of equal rights, a considerable number of people living in our world have not significantly improved their lot or achieved legal, economic or cultural parity. The economic, political and cultural disadvantages suffered by these outcasts are serious violations of justice.

Jesus is sending out a clear signal that we all have an urgent need to respond in faith and compassion to those on the margins, condemned to the exile of solitude by the forces of poverty and indifference. From that moment on, any desire to understand their plight must be informed by the gospel. If we are serious about our commitment to faith, then we must be committed to the oppressed.

Home for Christmas

At Mass on the Sunday before Christmas there was a crush of people. Christmas was a time of delirious reunions, as trains and buses to Athlone and Roscommon brought husbands, fathers, daughters, sons, girlfriends and boyfriends home to the bosom of their families.

Emigration was central to the culture of the west of Ireland. Communities were stripped of their young people in the same way a flock of sheep would demolish a field of fresh grass. It shaped the way people thought and felt, conditioning them to accept the grotesquely abnormal as normal. That was the way it was and that was the way it would always be. Although there were no industries, there was one highly developed export: people.

There were many scenes of families travelling en masse to the train station. Everyone wore their Sunday best. The mother was blind with tears. The father's eyes were dry, but his heart was breaking. Men did not betray emotion – it would have been seen as a sign of weakness. The young people leaving leaned out of the window, choking with sadness as they saw their parents for perhaps the last time. Younger brothers and sisters raced after the train shouting words of parting. Sometimes white handkerchiefs were produced and waved until the train went out of sight. Those handkerchiefs gave a ritual, almost sacramental, solemnity to the goodbyes. Their presence was a symbol of defeat, a damning indictment of an economy unable to provide for its brightest and most talented.

Hundreds of young and not so young people left every year. The collective tale of woe concealed thousands of individual nightmares. Young people wanted to stay in the country they loved, but had no way of making a living. They wanted to be close to family and friends, but they had no other choice but to leave. Many had good skills. Some had excellent examination results. Yet the piece of paper that was most important was the ticket to America. The shadow of emigration lurked like a vulture hovering over its prey. It was the traditional Irish solution to economic problems. It churned out an assembly line of bodies for the boat to England and America.

The clean-up

The day before Christmas Eve a great clean-up began and every room in the house was turned upside down and inside out as if very special visitors were coming. Everything was dusted, swept, scrubbed, scoured or polished, curtains were washed, and great piles of sticks were chopped and stored in the shed. On this day more than any other I marvelled at the hand of God in the Roscommon countryside. William Butler Yeats had a keen appreciation of this insight: 'Everything we look upon is blest.'

The twenty-fourth was the day when we finished our four thousand Hail Marys, which we had begun on the first day of Advent. I always began my season by faithfully saying my daily quota of 156 Hail Marys, but I inevitably let the practice slip in the middle of the month, and then in the final few days I had to bombard the heavens with prayers.

When the rosary was said, the children were dispatched to an early night in bed; no dissenting voices were raised. The back door remained unlocked whatever the weather, so that there was no danger of Mary and Joseph going astray in their search for a resting place.

High hopes

Although I was physically like my father, I inherited many of my grandfather's characteristics and qualities. The gap of two generations between us did not seem to matter. Whenever it was necessary he had no hesitation in bringing me down a peg or two, but criticism was always tactfully offered. In the cosseting comfort of his presence, I learned much about patience, kindness, and selflessness.

Part of my world collapsed when I heard that he died after an illness. His funeral will live with me forever: friends and family gathering for an occasion almost unbearably sad; a centre of my life gone. I was near to tears and in my heart there was something stirring: a sense of outrage, a feeling of total despair. I could not bring myself to think of him in the past tense, but I had seen the evidence of this the previous night as he lay in his coffin. He seemed so calm as he smiled and held his rosary beads in his hand. I hoped fervently that his soul had been set free from its anguish and that he would find peace at last in a higher, more perfect world.

Absent friends

Over twenty years on, his absence has become a presence. I miss him most on Christmas morning. To compensate, I recreate the journey we always took through the fields to feed the cattle and become entangled in the clinging cobwebs of childhood. In the softness of the western mist, as I walk these fields from which my heart can never be departed, I see his face. This land opens questions, often troubling questions, about my history and identity and goes even further to some secret compass point which directs me to somewhere I do not know – crossing boundaries where sadness and pain meet so dramatically. As I walk in this field I try to listen to its secrets of lives gained and lives lost, strange riches and sadness. It has a music of its own. The melody which enters my consciousness is a tune of loneliness, poignant cries of quiet despair. In these fields, people long dead live again, somehow speaking to years that belong to people not yet born. The ghost of my grandfather will always linger in these fields.

In Karl Rahner's magical phrase, Christmas is a time when 'grace is in the air'. To most people it is a celebration of the birth of Jesus, but for me it is tied to the memory of the death of my grandfather. Christmas Day is the best reminder to us that the eternal life to which we pray to be resurrected has begun long ago in a stable in Bethlehem. That is the real Christmas Presence.

Afterword: A Christmas Reflection
by Peter McVerry

It's all very confusing

There is a homeless person sitting in the street, begging. Passing by, I wonder whether to give him money or not. On the one hand, I feel sorry for him: no place to go, hungry, cold, bored. On the other hand, maybe he isn't really homeless, or even if he is, maybe he wants money for drugs or alcohol and I am actually making his situation worse by giving him money. It's all very confusing.

In the Millennium, a sustained campaign was waged to abolish or reduce the debt owed by the poorest Third World countries, which were being crippled by the interest they had to pay on loans they had received from the economically developed world. The campaigners argued that this repayment was preventing health and education programmes from being funded and was therefore costing lives and preventing development. Others argued that corruption was so extensive in many of these countries, and spending on arms and military was so high, that to simply cancel the debt would make their ruling elites even wealthier, their armies even better equipped and would thereby increase the oppression and suffering of the people, not reduce it. It's all very confusing.

Compassion

Unfortunately, ethical principles, while important, are not a quick-fix solution to our confusions. If they were, there would be no problems in the world. How do we build a more just world, where everyone's human rights and freedoms are respected? Ethical principles must be grounded in the values of compassion and solidarity. What is absent in our world today is not a set of ethical guidelines, but a deep sense of compassion and solidarity. Unless a person is living those values, unless a nation is living by those values, then ethical principles become, not guidelines to just behaviour, but lifeless rules to be manipulated, interpreted and twisted to one's own advantage.

Compassion is not a religious feeling. While it is central to many religious faiths, including Christianity, compassion is a human feeling that is innate to all of us. It is part of our humanity. Religious faith takes all that is most human in us and seeks to root it in an understanding and experience of a Creator God, who calls us into a relationship with that God. Compassion precedes faith. All of us, of whatever faith or none, are moved by the sight of children starving, or being ill-treated. Cruelty and sadism shock us all. We can, of course, become anaesthetised to suffering and cruelty and I think this is increasingly happening in our society. Technology has enabled us to witness the suffering of so many people in so many parts of our world that we sometimes close our eyes, because the pain becomes too much. We are also tempted to close our eyes because we feel so powerless to do anything about the pain – there is nothing worse than feeling pain at the suffering of another and knowing that we can do nothing about it. When there are only a few homeless people on the streets of our cities, we can reach out and show that we care, in different ways. But when there are so many homeless people, we tend to protect ourselves from our inability to reach out to all by shutting our eyes and our hearts. Compassion involves a desire to remove the pain from people's lives and give them a happier future. But when the pain of observing the pain of others becomes too much for us to bear, then we preserve our own sanity by switching off.

And so today we have lost not so much our compassion, but *our sense of outrage*. For the first time in Ireland since the Famine, there are today whole families living on the street because we have no accommodation for them. And yet we can spend €100 million on replacing a set of traffic lights at Newlands Cross in Clondalkin with a free flow junction, so that we can shorten our journey from Dublin to Cork by ten minutes. The Government can put aside €130 million to refund those who have paid their water charges, in the hope that it might help them to be re-elected. We are all aware of children dying in our world from hunger and preventable disease. But where is the anger, where is the indignation, where is the sense of outrage? Ethical principles must be rooted in a deep sense of compassion, a compassion that is sometimes expressed in anger. Compassion and anger are two sides of the same coin: you cannot love someone who is suffering unnecessarily without being angry at what is causing that suffering. To act ethically, we have to continually struggle against the tendency to numb the pain of seeing others in pain.

Solidarity

However, compassion is not enough. We are called to go further. To go beyond compassion to *solidarity*.

What does it mean to move beyond compassion to solidarity? There are two limitations to compassion. The first is that in compassion we tend to give from our *excess*: it is our surplus resources, our surplus time, our surplus energy that we devote to those in need. We may decide to give a donation to a charity, or we may decide to spend some of our time working with people on the margins. Irish people have, deservedly, a wonderful reputation for compassion. The contributions of the people of Ireland to disasters such as tsunamis or earthquakes are amongst the highest in the world per head of population. I, too, experience the compassion of Irish people for young homeless people, whose plight touches their hearts and makes them aware of how fortunate their own children have been. Our work is largely funded by their compassion. But the first limitation of compassion is that *we* decide what we will give to those in need.

The second limitation is that *we* decide to whom we will show compassion. *We* choose the people or charities we will support, judging them to be more or less deserving. Our compassion may stir someone to donate generously to a charity which provides counselling services for people who suffered sexual abuse as children, but we may decide that we will not contribute to a charity that is working with ex-prisoners, presumably because we do not consider that ex-prisoners deserve our charity – even though many are in prison in Ireland today because they were unable to cope with their experience of childhood sexual abuse! Those to whom we show compassion may be chosen quite arbitrarily (such as meeting a homeless person who is begging on the street) or may be chosen for us by the media (such as the image of a child crying who has lost their parents in a tsunami or earthquake). We reach out in compassion because their suffering has touched our hearts. Our compassion is, then, a feeling of distress at the pain and suffering of another human being and a desire to do something to alleviate it, usually something concrete and immediate.

But if we wish to transform our society or our world, the challenge for us is to move beyond compassion to solidarity.

Solidarity is a radical expression of compassion. Solidarity is rooted not in transient *feelings* of distress at the pain of others, but in a lifelong *commitment* to alleviating the pain of others. Solidarity derives not from our sense of generosity but from our sense of justice, from an acknowledgement that we are all united in our common humanity and the pain of others is our responsibility.

Solidarity, then, goes beyond compassion in two ways:

In compassion, *we* choose both those whom we will support, and how, and at what cost, we will support them. In solidarity, we do not choose either the victims or our response – *both are chosen for us*.

First, *we* no longer decide to whom we will reach out. Solidarity is a reaching out to *all* in our world who are victims, who are poor and who are marginalised, whether we like them or not, whether we feel threatened by them or not, whether we judge them to be deserving or not. It is the suffering of others that calls us into solidarity, not the choices we make.

Secondly, our response to the suffering of others is chosen not by us, but by those who suffer. Solidarity is a radical commitment to do whatever is required to alleviate their suffering, at whatever cost to ourselves.

Thus, our *compassion* for those who are homeless may bring us to donate generously to an appeal by a charity for homeless people – which will undoubtedly do a lot of good and alleviate a lot of suffering – but we may at the same time oppose the opening of a hostel for homeless people in our neighbourhood, on the grounds that our neighbourhood is not a suitable location for such a project.

Our *solidarity* with those who are homeless, however, may bring us to support such a project, if it is in the interests of homeless people, despite the cost (real or imagined) to ourselves, or to our property values. Solidarity compels us to support policies in favour of the poor which may be detrimental to our own interests.

Solidarity is a willingness to respond to the suffering of others with a love which is prepared to see *my* life changed, even radically, in order to bring change to those who suffer. The ultimate expression of solidarity is to be willing to lay down my life in order to bring life to others. It is a recognition that my concern for others is also, ultimately, a concern for myself; that *my* good cannot be achieved independently of *your* good; that in neglecting others, I am also diminishing myself. As the African proverb says: *If your neighbour is hungry, your chickens aren't safe.*

Compassion seeks to *alleviate* poverty and suffering in our world; but solidarity seeks to *eliminate* poverty and suffering.

Our sense of solidarity with others can help to prevent the anaesthetic from dulling the pain. To empathise with another person in their pain, to feel that pain as if it was our own, can help to keep us alert to the suffering in the world. It is John, Mary and Jane's pain – John, Mary and Jane being persons known to us – which helps to minimise the tendency to treat the suffering of others as merely a 'problem'. It helps to prevent the anonymity of others, others being considered objectively as the 'clients' and the problem being 'an issue'. We need to get to know people who are poor, suffering and marginalised, to be able to see life through their eyes. People who are waiting years for an operation may see the budget in a very different way to those who are cushioned by their VHI payments. Preserving our sense of outrage through personal, direct contact with *some* people who are poor, suffering or marginalised makes it more likely that we will act ethically towards *all* those who are poor.

> Solidarity is not a feeling of vague compassion or shallow distress at the misfortunes of so many people, both near and far. On the contrary, it is a firm and persevering determination to commit oneself to the common good: that is to say, to the good of all and of each individual because we are all really responsible for all.
>
> Encyclical 'Social Concern', par. 38

This was my own experience when I started working in the inner city of Dublin in 1974. I went to live there with two other Jesuits in the old tenement buildings. Each house was divided into eight flats. Two things shocked me. First, the conditions in which people lived there were appalling. We had a top floor flat – luckily when we moved in it wasn't raining. The place was crawling with rats, and the rats were the size of little kittens and immune to every poison that was ever invented. In our flat on the top floor, you just listened all night to the rats running on the ceiling, fighting each other, squealing, dragging bits of food. But on the ground floor, or the first floor, parents would tell you of waking up in the morning and finding a rat on the baby's cot.

But that wasn't the worst of it. The worst of it was that there was no soundproofing between flats, as they were originally only rooms in a large house. We could hear the news on the TV in the flat below us perfectly clearly. Now, each house had at least one family with problems, and the problems were usually drink related. In our house the family with problems lived in the flat below us. Both parents were alcoholics who spent the evening in the pub and, about three times a week, came home at 1 a.m. and had an almighty row. They would be shouting and roaring at each other, cups would fly across the room and smash against the wall, and you would hear their three-year-old child crying in one of the bedrooms. This row would go on for maybe two hours, until they fell asleep from drink and exhaustion. But the rest of the house was wide awake – you didn't sleep through this. So, imagine parents who had to get up in the morning to go to work. Frequently they wouldn't get to sleep until three or four in the morning, so they would sleep it out in the morning and arrive into work late. So, the employer would eventually get fed up and sack them. And imagine children who had to get up to go to school. Again, they would get into school late and sit at the back of the class dozing off; gradually they would lose interest in school and either leave or get expelled for disruptive behaviour.

It was impossible to go to school; at that time, no child had ever gone to school in that area after the age of twelve. As a result they were hanging around the street all day and half the night. Most of their parents were unemployed and couldn't give them any pocket money, so what were they doing? A little bit of robbing. And by the time they were sixteen or seventeen, they were doing a lot of robbing and going to prison. It was as predictable as day follows night.

But what shocked me even more than the conditions which hundreds of families had to endure in this area was the fact that I had been living in Dublin for the previous twenty years, and had walked through this area regularly, but the housing conditions in which people had to live did not impact on me at all. Yes, I was aware that the conditions were bad, and thought it was unfortunate that people had to live there. Yet it was only when I went to live there, to experience the conditions myself, and to befriend people who had no choice but to live there, that I became outraged by it all and determined to do what little I could to change it.

If our solidarity is to be 'a firm and persevering determination to commit oneself to the common good', it needs to be rooted in that personal contact with some people on the margins.

It goes similarly with our politicians and decision makers. If we are to build a just society, they too need to be in constant, direct contact with homeless people, drug users, prisoners, people in poor neighbourhoods. It is not sufficient to meet 'clients' in their clinics. Indeed, meeting 'clients' in their clinics can convince them that they know the problems which they face. But like me walking through the inner city, I had a 'head' knowledge of the problems, but no 'heart' knowledge, and only the 'heart' knowledge moves us to action.

Jesus did not pronounce ethical principles; he told stories about people, which enthused his listeners and outraged them.

He told the story of the rich man who was dressed in the finest clothes and feasted sumptuously every day. And the poor man who sat at his gate, hoping to get a few crumbs from the rich man's table. But the rich man couldn't be bothered (Lk 16:9-26).

He told the story of the rich landowner who had a bumper harvest, and wondered what to do with his record crop. 'I know,' he said, 'I will build bigger barns and store up my produce there and I will have enough to last me for the rest of my life' – without sparing a thought for the hungry and poor all around him.

He told the story of the workers in the market places who waited there each day to see if someone would hire them and give them a wage which would allow them to feed their family that day. If they didn't get hired, their family went hungry.

His stories talked about situations in which people were treated badly, ignored or walked upon. These were not made-up stories – they were real-life stories with which many of his listeners would be familiar. The stories enabled people to empathise with others in the unjust situation in which they found themselves. The ethical thing to do was usually very clear, the ethical principles were deafeningly loud, but Jesus explained them in terms of concrete situations and real people. The discernment demanded by Jesus was based on compassion and solidarity:

> So always treat others as you would like them to treat you; that is the meaning of the Law and the Prophets.
>
> Mt 7:12

Self-deception

Ethical principles have to struggle against our almost infinite capacity for self-deception. Our ability to rationalise and make decisions which are in our own interests, while preserving the belief that we are acting ethically, is usually very apparent in others! However, we can often delude ourselves that this very common phenomenon does not affect us. Our desire for comfort or for security are two frequently occurring drives which affect the decisions we make. Our attachment to our own way of doing things, or our own attitudes and feelings about things, may prevent us from being objective. During the era of slavery, many God-fearing, good-living people owned slaves. Hopefully some of them treated their slaves well, as their ethical principles required. But these ethical principles often did not challenge the institution of slavery itself. This self-interest which clouds our objectivity is particularly difficult to unmask, as it may be rooted very deeply in one's psyche and therefore be hidden, even to one's self. Unjust structures, such as slavery, become embedded in our consciousness and we fail to see the injustice in them.

If I had grown up in Pakistan, I would not now be a Jesuit priest, but would probably be a Muslim Imam, or perhaps even a suicide bomber. If I had grown up in a staunch Unionist family, my mindset, my understanding of what is happening in society and the changes that are needed, would be very different to my mindset if I had grown up in a staunchly Republican family. If I had grown up in a Fianna Fáil family, well, there are some good counsellors around!

Most of us, however, believe that we are the essence of objectivity and are unwilling to admit that we are motivated by self-interest. The problem is not bad people making bad decisions, but good people making bad decisions having convinced themselves that they were good decisions. They are not acting out of malice – indeed it would be much easier to deal with them if they were! – but out of ignorance. Ignorance of the reality of life for poor people, and of the effect the decisions they make can have on their lives.

We see it in relations between different parts of the world, between different countries, different regions, different communities. Decisions that could make a vital, life-giving difference to some people are rejected, watered down, compromised because of the relatively minor effects or inconvenience which those decisions would have on those who make them.

A major part of the rationalisation which we all go on with is our inability, or unwillingness, to listen. We do not want our situation or our thinking to be disturbed by the contrary views of others. And so we set up mechanisms by which challenges can be dismissed. We find all sorts of reasons which invalidate or rubbish such views. This is especially true of the views of the poor themselves, which of course challenge us the most.

If I live in the top floor flat of a building and at eight o'clock in the morning I pull back the curtains, the sun shines in. I look out the window into the back garden and see the lovely multicoloured flowers swaying in the breeze and watch the birds dancing on the lawn looking for worms. It seems to be another wonderful day.

But if I live in the basement flat of the same building and at eight o'clock in the morning I pull back the curtains, nothing happens – the sun can't get in. I look out the window into the back garden and all I see is the whitewashed wall of the outside toilet – I cannot see the flowers or the birds or the lawn. I'm not sure what sort of day it is.

Here we have two people looking out of the same house into the same garden at the same time of the same day – and they have two totally different views: there is a view from the top and a view from the bottom.

In our society there are two (indeed more than two) totally different views. There is the view of those who are in well-paid, secure, pensionable jobs, living in a nice house in a nice area and whose children are going to third-level education; and there is the view of those who are living on the fourteenth floor of a tower block in Ballymun where the lifts don't work, who have been unemployed for twelve years and whose children have dropped out of school and are hanging around with wrong crowd. How they see the structures of Irish society, and how they view the political, economic and social decisions that are made, will probably be very different.

The perspective of the poor does not have any greater legitimacy than the perspective of any other group in our society or in our world. It is, like any other view, the view of a particular group who sees the world from their own unique situation. However, while it does not have greater legitimacy, it does have greater priority, simply because it is the view of those who are suffering or who have been excluded. This gives their viewpoint a uniqueness which demands particular attention. However, it often receives particular disdain – because they often lack education, and so they are written off as not having the knowledge to understand the 'complexity' of reality; or because they lack the literacy skills to present their views in a way that keeps decision makers happy; or because they are perceived to be biased because of their particular problems (as if the rest of us weren't!).

It is the difficult task of continually trying to listen to the views of those who are poor and excluded, of trying to see life as it were through their eyes, which sustains our compassion and our solidarity. It is difficult because it challenges us, our viewpoint, our securities; sometimes it even accuses us. And we usually do not like to be challenged, much less accused.

This season each of us must face the question: Will I be the Christmas Presence and show compassion and solidarity?

Food for Thought

I prefer a Church which is bruised, hurting and dirty because it has been out on the streets, rather than clinging to its own security.

Pope Francis, *Evangelii Gaudium*, par. 49

The Last Word

Truly the day was already far spent and the evening drawing near;
the sun of justice was already beginning to set,
and its rays now gave diminished light and warmth to the earth.
The light of the knowledge of God had grown feeble,
and as sin increased, charity grew cold.
Angels no longer appeared to men,
no prophet raised his voice;
it seemed as though, overcome by the great hardness and
obstinacy of men,
they had ceased to intervene in human affairs.

Then it was that the Son of God said: 'Here am I'.

Saint Bernard of Clairvaux, *First Sermon for Advent*

Acknowledgements

A very sincere and deep thanks to Peter McVerry for his enthusiastic support for this group from day one.

Very special thanks to the great Don Conroy for his wonderful illustrations. Thanks too to Sarah Conroy for her assistance.

I am profoundly grateful to Brian Flannery for his invaluable and very practical help for this project on behalf of 'the Jesuit family'.

As always I am very appreciative for the concrete support of my good friend John Littleton.

Siobhan O'Grady was very much in my mind as this book was written. I hope she will find that love is all around.

While this book was being written, Liz O'Brien was to the foremost of my thoughts following the sad loss of her beloved father.

In September we lost two much loved teachers Connell Doris and Christy Hannon. Two gentlemen and two good men.

Other sad losses were Ivor Dada and Cathy Burlingham, one of the great love stories of our time, leaving a treasure trove of happy memories for their children and grandchildren.

Thanks to Patrick and The Columba Press for their interest in this book.